Betty Crocker's

NEW
CHINESE
COOKBOOK

Recipes by
Leeann Chin

PRENTICE HALL

New York   London   Toronto   Sydney   Tokyo   Singapore

Prentice Hall
15 Columbus Circle
New York, NY 10023

Published simultaneously in Canada by Prentice Hall Canada, Inc.

PRENTICE HALL and colophon are registered trademarks
of Simon & Schuster Inc.

BETTY CROCKER is a registered trademark
of General Mills, Inc.

Library of Congress Cataloging-in-Publication Data

Chin, Leeann.
    Betty Crocker's New Chinese cookbook.—1st ed.
       p.   cm.
    Includes index.
    ISBN 0-13-083254-5
    1. Cookery, Chinese.   I. Crocker, Betty.   II. Title.
TX724.5.C5C56116   1990
641.5951—dc20   89-16053
                                    CIP

Manufactured in the United States of America

10 9 8 7 6 5 4 3 2 1

First Edition

Credits

PRENTICE HALL

Vice-President and Publisher: Anne M. Zeman
Senior Editor: Rebecca W. Atwater
Art Director: Laurence Alexander
Assistant Art Director: Patricia Fabricant
Photography Designer: Frederick J. Latasa
Text Designer: Amy Barison Cohen
Prop Stylist: IDESIGN
Illustrator: Lauren Jarrett
Production Editor: John L. Bottomley
Production Manager: Susan Joseph
Editorial Assistant: Rachel A. Simon

GENERAL MILLS, INC.

Editor: Lois Tlusty
Copy Editor: Judy Anderson
Editorial Assistant: Pamela Jones
Food Stylists: Katie W. McElroy, Cindy Lund, Carol Grones
Photographer: Nanci E. Doonan
Photography Assistant: Chuck Carver
Director, Betty Crocker Food and Publication Center:
Marcia Copeland
Assistant Manager, Publications: Lois Tlusty

Quality Printing and Binding by
The Lakeside Press
R.R. Donnelley & Sons Company
Willard Manufacturing Division
1145 Conwell Avenue
Willard, Ohio 44888-9462
U.S.A.

CONTENTS

FOREWORD

You don't have to be Chinese to enjoy Chinese cooking, but it helps to learn how to cook Chinese from someone who is. One of the world's most popular cuisines, Chinese cooking is perfect for today's hectic and health-conscious lifestyle. This revised collection of recipes brings you many new, refreshing dishes—Chicken-Papaya Salad and Marinated Mushrooms and Cucumbers, for example—as well as the restaurant favorites you have always longed to cook at home.

Turn to Chinese Cooking Basics and you'll be amazed to discover how simple this exotic food is to prepare. Restaurateur and Chinese chef Leeann Chin leads you through the techniques and explains the ingredients that make this type of cooking just about irresistible. Most of the cooking is done in minutes, too, and many of our recipes have reduced oil. For those concerned about salt intake, try low-sodium soy sauce; it has 40 percent less sodium, and we'll bet you can't taste the difference.

Leeann Chin created these recipes with simplicity and authenticity in mind. Born in Canton, China, she moved to the United States as a young adult. Today she is famous as a cook, teacher, and proprietor of three stylish Chinese restaurants and nine carryout locations as well as prosperous catering and conference facilities.

Unique flavorings and techniques make Chinese cooking intrinsically intriguing; a tradition that emphasizes quality over quantity lets you use inexpensive ingredients or small amounts of expensive ones. You'll find that the flavors are so intense, a little goes a long way, making it practical for everyday as well as appropriate for very special occasions. If you have never cooked Chinese food before, you might start by preparing one or two dishes and serving them as part of western-style meals. As you become more experienced with Chinese cooking techniques, you will be able to serve authentic Chinese meals with ease.

THE BETTY CROCKER EDITORS

CHINESE COOKING BASICS

China is a nation steeped in more than 5,000 years of history; few realize that its culinary heritage has been developed and perfected for this length of time as well. Perhaps through isolation—the country is enclosed by the world's highest mountains, a vast desert and the Great Wall—the Chinese have developed an artful style of cooking that, with patience and attention to detail, achieves simplicity, balance and harmony.

It takes some time to prepare recipe ingredients, but very little time to cook them, and in the end, the result is something that pleases all the senses. Chinese food is pleasing to the eye because it has attractive color and shape. It is fragrant with the aroma of fresh ginger, lemon or garlic; it contrasts sweet and sour, hot and cold, and smooth and crunchy. It tantalizes us with the explosion of cellophane noodles when they are immersed in hot oil. The flavor may be exquisitely subtle or rousingly bold.

Chinese meals strive for balance, both nutritionally and aesthetically. A typical meal includes rice, soup and one dish from each of the following groups: meat, fish, poultry and vegetables. All dishes served at a traditional Chinese meal are prepared in different styles (stir-fried, deep-fried or steamed), and all have equal importance; none is the "main" dish.

As important as a balanced meal or balance among the dishes is the desire to expose contrasts. Cold dishes usually begin a banquet, hot dishes follow. One dish may be smooth, another crisp; one dish may highlight color, while another displays dark and light or even pale ingredients. Textures, too, within a dish may vary. Smooth tofu may be served with crunchy lotus root or water chestnuts. But as with the opposites yin and yang, there is harmony.

There are no hard-and-fast rules with Chinese cooking. You can be as creative as you like, with no limit to the number of dishes you can prepare with the fresh produce you may have on hand or can find in most markets. You need no special equipment, just a few sharp knives, a spatula or two, plenty of bowls and a good skillet or Dutch oven, if you don't own a wok.

Much of Chinese cuisine uses oil and salt (or salty ingredients such as soy sauce, bean sauce and dried seafood). Many of the recipes in this collection have reduced the amount of oil needed, but a nonstick skillet or wok can reduce the oil even further. If salt is a concern, look for low-sodium soy sauces. You might also consider omitting the second amount of salt for seasoning if you use canned broths, which contain a considerable amount of salt.

Sichuan Chicken with Cashews (page 52)

1

COOKING METHODS

Chinese cooking embraces the three ways most foods are cooked: in oil or water or with dry heat. The techniques are known as stir-frying, deep-frying and steaming (roasting is done mostly in restaurants, because few families have ovens).

STIR-FRYING. Stir-frying dates to the early days when Chinese families cooked on small, portable wood-burning stoves that produced intense flames over which food cooked quickly. The wok, designed for stir-frying, allows for maximum distribution of heat from a minimum amount of fuel. The ingredients are cut into uniformly small pieces so they cook rapidly.

Stir-frying cooks food in a small amount of oil. Ingredients are added sequentially and are stirred vigorously over high heat so that everything is cooked at the same time. The hot oil seals in flavors and colors, enriches the food and gives it a shiny appearance.

Always begin stir-frying with a clean, dry wok. Heat the wok over high heat before adding oil, then tilt it to coat the interior so the food won't stick. Add a slice of gingerroot to the oil to test if it is hot enough. If it sizzles, the oil is ready.

Successful stir-frying depends on the intensity of the heat, timing the addition of ingredients and the correct quantity of ingredients. Ordinary home-cooked meals would include only one stir-fried dish. Remember that tougher ingredients such as broccoli require longer cooking times and should be added first, while tender ingredients require less time and should be added last. It is easy to tell when stir-fried food is cooked because it changes color. Thinly sliced chicken and pork turn white and beef is no longer red. Vegetables are a brighter color but are still crisp.

When stir-frying, use quick, downward strokes to keep the food moving. Use a spatula with a firm base; slip it down the side of the wok and across the bottom, turning the food over. Use one hand to stir and the other to hold onto the wok. If food sticks or if moisture seeps from the food, either the wok is not hot enough or too much food is being cooked at once. If that is the case, remove the food to a separate bowl, wash and thoroughly dry the wok and proceed with the next step. Always organize and arrange the ingredients in the order in which they are needed. This will help avoid overcooking some foods and undercooking others. For best results, use vegetable and peanut oil; they tolerate high heat. Margarine and butter should not be used because they burn.

DEEP-FRYING. Deep-frying involves immersing batter-dipped pieces of meat, fish, poultry or vegetables in hot oil. Sometimes the pieces are marinated before they are dipped for more intense flavor. Food is deep-fried in two steps: first it is fried to a golden brown, then drained and cooled. The oil is reheated and the food is fried a second time. The two-stage method ensures that the food is fully cooked, with a crisp exterior; it prevents the outside from overcooking before the inside is done. Woks, with their deep, rounded shapes, are ideal for deep-frying. Deep, heavy saucepans or Dutch ovens work just as well.

To deep-fry, pour in the correct amount of oil and heat uncovered (to prevent overheating). Use a deep-fat thermometer to check the temperature of the oil at regular intervals during cooking. If the temperature is too high, the food will brown on the outside before the inside is done. If it is not hot enough, the food will sink and become greasy. Remove each batch of deep-fried food from the hot oil with a fine wire strainer. Let the oil return to the recommended temperature before continuing with the next batch. If the oil overheats, turn off the burner until the oil cools.

Oil can be reused after deep-frying, but it must be clarified and properly stored. Line a wire strainer with several layers of cheesecloth and place it in a bowl. Pour the cooled oil through the strainer, and store it in a clean, tightly covered bottle in the refrigerator. If the oil has been used to cook fish, brown three or four pieces of gingerroot in it to remove traces of the fish flavor. Discard the gingerroot, let the oil cool and proceed as directed above.

STEAMING. Steaming is used for meats, fish, poultry, dumplings and rice. Traditionally, food is placed in a bamboo steamer, which is covered and set in a wok. Boiling water is added to just within ½ inch of the bottom of the bamboo steamer; the steamer is covered and then heated. (The amount of water used in our recipes will produce steam over high heat for about fifteen to twenty-five minutes.) You can also use a metal or a wooden rack placed in a wok, Dutch oven or electric skillet as a substitute for the bamboo steamer. Place the food on a heatproof plate or bowl on the rack and cover the plate with a tight-fitting lid that will allow for the steam to circulate in the one or two inches of air space above the food.

You can improvise a steamer or rack by using empty cans, inverted heatproof bowls or chopsticks in the bottom of the wok, Dutch oven or skillet. Place the food on a heatproof plate and set the plate on the empty cans. Fill the wok with boiling water to ½ inch of the top of the cans and inverted bowls or to within ½ inch to the bottom of the plate and cover the plate tightly. Be sure to check the water level during steaming; add boiling water if necessary, but pour it down the side of the wok so that it does not touch the food.

BLANCHING. Blanching is the brief immersion of vegetables in boiling water to partially cook them. Blanching preserves their color, texture and flavor. To blanch, place prepared vegetables in a wire strainer with a long handle; lower the strainer into boiling water and cover. Tender vegetables such as Chinese pea pods should be blanched approximately thirty

seconds, or until the water returns to a boil. Tougher vegetables such as broccoli and cauliflower may take up to two minutes. After the vegetables have been removed, they should be rinsed under cold running water to stop the cooking.

CUTTING

Whenever possible, the Chinese try to achieve "harmony of cut," which means all the ingredients will be cut the same. For example, in Shrimp Almond Ding, all the ingredients are diced into small cubes that resemble the size of the peas in the recipe. If the main ingredient of a recipe is shredded, then so are the lesser ingredients. Most stir-fries require thinly sliced meats and vegetables, deep-fries require diced pieces that will remain firm after the immersion in hot oil, and steamed ingredients (with the exception of fish or poultry) are minced.

It is very important to know how to cut correctly. Your cleaver or knife should always be clean and very sharp. The hand holding the food should always have the fingertips hold the food securely on the cutting surface and with fingers curled so knuckles almost touch the blade of the knife. The knuckles act as a guide for the blade. Gradually move

the hand back while cutting. It is a safe guide-line not to lift the cutting edge of the blade higher than the knuckles of the hand holding the food unless the fingers are safely out of the way.

SLICING MEAT. It is easier to slice meat that has been in the freezer about fifteen minutes or just until it is firm but not frozen.

Cut meat lengthwise, with the grain, into strips about two inches wide. Cut each strip across the grain into ⅛-inch strips.

SLICING CELERY AND BOK CHOY

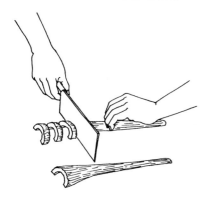

Cut straight across at the widest end of the stalk.

Cut across the stalk at an angle as the stalk narrows.

DIAGONAL SLICING

Keep the blade at an angle to the cutting surface.

DICING AND CUBING

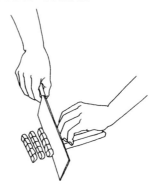

Cut meat or vegetables into strips less than ½ inch wide for dicing, wider for cubing. Hold strips together and cut into pieces as long as they are wide.

SHREDDING

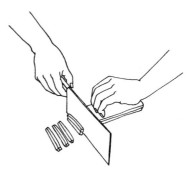

Cut meat or vegetables into 2 × ⅛-inch slices. Stack the slices; cut lengthwise into thin strips.

CHINESE UTENSILS

It isn't necessary to purchase any special implements to prepare Chinese food. A few sharp knives, skillets, saucepans, a Dutch oven, turners and strainers will suffice. If you prepare Chinese food frequently, consider cookware with a nonstick surface. You can use a nonstick pan for meats, a wok for vegetables. Traditional Chinese cookware includes

CHOPSTICKS. Chopsticks are known as "quick little ones." They are used for eating, cooking and stirring ingredients, and they are said to represent extensions of the thumb and first finger. Plastic, lacquered or ivory chopsticks are used for eating, while bamboo and wooden ones are used for cooking; they don't melt or bend from the heat as the others do. Different in shape from Japanese chopsticks, Chinese chopsticks are longer and less tapered, with blunt tips.

SPATULA. The spatula used by the Chinese has a long bamboo or wooden handle and a slightly curved edge that fits the shape of the wok. With its slight lip, the spatula can hold sauces. A pancake turner works just as well.

LADLE. The ladle is shallow and bowl shaped, with a long bamboo or wooden handle. It is used to remove food from woks, but a large serving spoon is adequate.

WIRE LADLE AND STRAINER. The wire ladle is really a wire mesh scoop with a long, flat bamboo or wooden handle. It is used primarily to remove food from broth or oil. The fine mesh strainer removes those bits of food that would otherwise burn if they were left in hot oil.

CLEAVER. Cleavers come in different sizes. The most useful has a blade three to four inches wide and about eight inches long. Large, heavy cleavers ("bone knives") are used to chop meat, including the bone; few Chinese preparations call for the meat and bone to be separated. Thinner cleavers are used to slice meat and vegetables.

STEAMER. Traditional Chinese steamers are made of bamboo. They are shaped like round baskets with woven bottoms and lids and rest on the curved sides of the wok. When reheating, more than one steamer may be stacked in a wok. When steam cooking, don't stack. Steamers vary in size from four inches in diameter, for cooking dim sum, to sixteen inches in diameter, for cooking seafood and poultry. A ten-inch diameter steamer is the most versatile.

WOK. Woks were designed for stir-frying, to shorten cooking time and save fuel. They are an all-purpose cooking utensil, perfect for deep-frying, steaming or stewing food.

The wok easiest to use is 14 to 16 inches in diameter. Woks are made of rolled carbon steel, aluminum or stainless steel. There are also electric woks and woks with nonstick finishes. The carbon steel woks are the traditional Chinese versions. They were developed to heat quickly and evenly and to save fuel; they require special care. To "season" a carbon steel wok, wash it with hot, soapy water and dry it on your stove over medium heat. Rub about 2 teaspoons of vegetable oil evenly over the inside of the wok, using a soft cloth. Repeat the process if food sticks during stir-frying.

Aluminum and stainless steel woks require no seasoning, but they do not heat as evenly as carbon steel. Because they do not rust, they are a good choice for steaming foods. Electric woks are also convenient. Be sure to follow the manufacturer's directions for their care and use.

GLOSSARY
OF INGREDIENTS

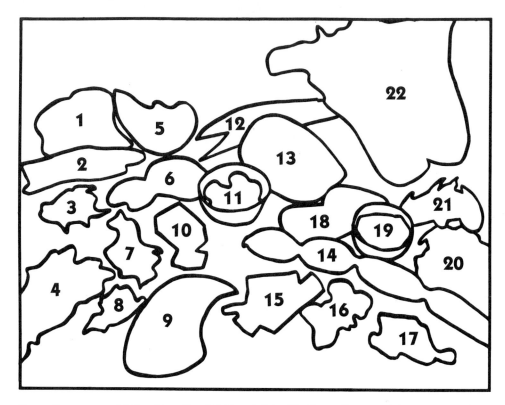

Preceding pages: (*1*) Egg Noodles (*2*) Rice Sticks (*3*) Tiger Lily Buds (*4*) Gingerroot (*5*) Winter Melon (*6*) Jicama (*7*) Green Chilies (*8*) Pickled Gingerroot (*9*) Fresh Rice Noodles (*10*) Tofu (*11*) Water Chestnuts (*12*) White Radish (*13*) Chinese Cabbage (*14*) Lotus Root (*15*) Bamboo Shoots (*16*) Dried Black Mushrooms (*17*) Straw Mushrooms (*18*) Cellophane Noodles (*19*) Salted Black Beans (*20*) Bean Sprouts (*21*) Chinese Pea Pods (*22*) Bok Choy

BAMBOO SHOOTS. The young, tender, ivory-colored shoots from the tropical bamboo plant are eaten as a vegetable. They can be purchased whole, sliced or in chunks, or water packed in cans. The tender, pointed end of the shoot is used for stir-frying. The wide, less tender end is used for soups and stews or can be sliced very thin for stir-frying. Refrigerate bamboo shoots covered with cold water in a tightly covered jar. Change the water daily.

BEAN SPROUTS. Young, white sprouts of the mung bean have a crisp texture and delicate flavor. Bean sprouts can be found fresh or canned. Just prior to cooking, they should be rinsed in cold water to retain their crispness. Keep them covered with cold water in a covered container in the refrigerator; use them within four days.

BLACK BEANS, SALTED. (Black fermented beans). Small, black fermented soybeans have a strong, pungent, salty flavor. Salted black beans are sold in jars, cans or plastic bags of various sizes. Stir the beans in warm water for 2 minutes, then drain well, to remove excess salt. Refrigerate, tightly covered, after opening. Brown bean sauce can be substituted.

BOK CHOY. (Chinese chard or white mustard cabbage). This vegetable resembles both chard and cabbage, with crisp, white stalks and shiny, dark green leaves. It is used primarily in soups and stir-fried dishes. The leaves are easily separated from the stalks and should be added last to dishes to avoid overcooking. Bok choy is sold by the pound.

BROWN BEAN SAUCE. (Brown bean paste). A thick, salty sauce made from fermented yellow soybeans, flour and salt, brown bean sauce adds flavor to cooked meats or sauces. It is purchased whole or ground in cans, jars or plastic packages. Whole beans should be mashed before using. Refrigerate, tightly covered, after opening. Dark soy sauce can be substituted.

CELERY CABBAGE. (Napa cabbage, Chinese cabbage or sui choy). The dense, oblong heads of celery cabbage feature long, smooth stalks with pale green leaves.

CHILIES. When selecting green chilies, look for glossy, plump unblemished ones. Hot green chilies can be hot peppers, jalpeños or serranos, to name the more common ones. The degree of heat will vary from chili to chili due to growing conditions, so even the name of the chili is no guarantee of how hot it will taste. Chilies range from hot to incendiary, the smallest chilies being the hottest. Removing seeds and membranes will help to make the finished dish less hot (easily done with kitchen scissors). Handle chilies with caution—the volatile oils can burn eyes and other sensitive parts of the body. Wash hands and utensils with warm soapy water after handling chilies. Fresh chilies can be refrigerated for at least two weeks.

CHILI PASTE. (Chili paste with garlic, chili sauce or Sichuan paste). This hot, spicy sauce is made from soybeans, hot peppers, salt, oil and garlic. In Sichuan it is used both in cooking and as a condiment. Chili paste is imported from Hong Kong and Taiwan, sold in jars or bottles. Refrigerate, tightly covered, after opening. To make chili paste, heat an 8-inch skillet over medium-high heat until hot. Add 1 tablespoon vegetable oil. Stir in ¼ cup ground brown bean sauce, 1 teaspoon ground red pepper, 1 tablespoon sugar and 1 tablespoon finely chopped gingerroot. Reduce heat to low. Cook 10 minutes, stirring frequently so it does not burn.

CILANTRO. (Chinese parsley or fresh coriander). This strongly flavored, aromatic herb with broad, flat serrated leaves has citrus overtones. Sometimes a principal flavoring, it is often used as a garnish for both hot and cold dishes. There is no substitute.

COCONUT MILK. Coconut milk is available in cans at Oriental specialty stores and is made from coconut meat and water. Do not substitute sweetened coconut cream.

EGG ROLL SKINS. These paper-thin, soft square sheets of dough made from eggs, flour and water are used for wrapping meat, shrimp or vegetables, then are deep-fried. The sheets are sold frozen or refrigerated. Allow frozen egg roll skins to thaw completely.

FIVE-SPICE POWDER. (Five spices, five-flavored powder, five-fragrance spice powder or five-fragrance powder). This mixture of five ground spices is slightly sweet and pungent. Star anise, cinnamon and cloves are usually three of the five spices used. Store, tightly covered, in a dry place at room temperature.

GINGERROOT. One of the most basic seasonings in Chinese cooking, this gnarled brown root (about three inches long) can be refrigerated or frozen whole, sliced or chopped, but tightly wrapped. There is no acceptable substitute for fresh gingerroot in Chinese recipes.

GINGERROOT, PICKLED. These small amber knobs of young gingerroot are preserved in heavy syrup. Red sweet gingerroot, pieces of bright red ginger in a heavy syrup, can be substituted. Pickled gingerroot is available in jars at Oriental specialty stores and will keep indefinitely, as long as syrup covers the gingerroot.

GINGERROOT JUICE. To make it, press thin slices of fresh gingerroot in a garlic press. Or, squeeze finely chopped gingerroot between fingers to extract the juice.

HOISIN SAUCE. (Hoisen, hoison, haisein or Peking sauce). This thick, sweet reddish brown sauce usually made from soybeans, vinegar, chilies, spices and garlic is used in cooking and as a table condiment. Refrigerate tightly after opening. There is no substitute.

JICAMA. This brown-skinned root vegetable has a crunchy, sweet white interior. It will keep in the refrigerator for several weeks. Water chestnuts can be substituted in salads.

LOTUS ROOT. Available fresh and canned in Oriental specialty stores, lotus root is a long potatolike root vegetable with a creamy colored interior. Refrigerate fresh and canned after opening. There is no substitute.

MUSHROOMS, DRIED BLACK. (Chinese dried mushrooms, dried Chinese mushrooms, black dried mushrooms, winter mushrooms). With intense mushroom flavor, these have caps that vary in size from ½ to 2 inches in diameter. They must be soaked in water until tender, then rinsed free of grit before using. Store, tightly covered, at room temperature. Fresh mushrooms or straw mushrooms may be substituted in stir-fry recipes only.

MUSHROOMS, STRAW. (Grass mushrooms). These tender, mushrooms about 1½ to 2 inches tall with long leaflike caps are sold fresh, canned or dried. Soak the dried mushrooms and wash many times in water before using. Refrigerate the canned mushrooms covered with water after opening.

NOODLES, CELLOPHANE. (Bean threads, shining noodles, transparent noodles or vermicelli). These brittle, white noodles made from mung beans become translucent, soft and gelatinous when they absorb liquid, puffy and crisp when deep fried. They are sold in cellophane packages. Fried rice stick noodles may be substituted for fried cellophane noodles.

NOODLES, EGG. This alimentary pasta made of flour and eggs is available dried or frozen and is served pan fried or in soups. Thin egg noodles or spaghetti can be substituted.

OIL. Vegetable, peanut or corn oil can be used for deep-frying, stir-frying and marinating foods. Peanut oil has a higher smoking point but is somewhat more expensive than vegetable oil. Refrigerate oils after opening to prevent rancidity.

OIL, HOT. (Chili oil, sesame chili oil). This chili-pepper-infused cooking oil is fiery hot and excellent in dipping sauce. Commercially made hot oil has a tendency to go rancid quickly; homemade hot oil stored in the refrigerator will last much longer. To make hot oil, heat 8-inch skillet until hot. Add 3 tablespoons vegetable oil and 1 teaspoon cayenne pepper. Heat over medium heat 5 minutes. Remove from heat; let stand until cool. Pour through a strainer lined with a paper towel or paper coffee filter. Store, tightly covered, in the refrigerator.

RICE. There are two principal varieties of rice: long grain and short grain. Long grain rice is generally preferred for Chinese cooking because it is firmer when cooked. It should be washed in cold water until the water is clear to remove excess starch. Store rice at room temperature.

RICE STICK NOODLES. (Long rice or rice flour noodles). These thin, brittle white noodles made from rice powder must be softened in liquid before stir-frying. When deep-fried they become puffy and crisp and are used as a garnish. Rice sticks are sold in cellophane packages and stored at room temperature. Deep-fried cellophane noodles may be substituted for deep-fried rice stick noodles.

SICHUAN PRESERVED VEGETABLES. (Sichuan preserved radish, Sichuan preserved mustard stem or Szechuan preserved vegetables). This greenish knob is preserved in salt and chili powder. It has a hot and salty taste and is very crunchy. Diced, shredded or sliced, it is added to cooked dishes or used in cold dishes. The whole knob should be carefully washed to remove excess salt and any sand. It is available in cans or open crocks. It will keep in a tightly covered jar indefinitely.

SIU MAI SKINS. These are thin, soft 3½-inch circles of dough made from eggs, flour and water. They are used for dumplings and filled with meat, poultry or seafood mixtures to be steamed or boiled. Wonton skins can be substituted; remove the corners to form circles. Siu mai skins are sold frozen or refrigerated.

SOY SAUCE. This salty brown sauce is made from soybeans, wheat, yeast and salt. There are three types: light, dark and heavy. Light soy sauce—light in color and delicately flavored—is used in clear soups and in marinades. Dark soy sauce is made from the same ingredients as light, with the addition of caramel for a richer color. Both light and dark soy sauces can be used as table condiments. Heavy soy sauce is made with molasses and is thick and dark. It is used for color in dark sauces. Oriental imported soy sauces are preferred because they are made by a slow, natural process of fermentation and aging. Soy sauce is sold in bottles or cans and can be stored at room temperature.

SOY SAUCE, MUSHROOM. This soy sauce is flavored with mushrooms and a hint of sugar. It is dark and slightly thicker than regular soy sauce, delicious when added to stir-fried meat or vegetable dishes. It is sold in bottles and should be stored at room temperature.

SPRING ROLL SKINS. These paper-thin, translucent squares or rounds of dough are similar to egg roll skins. They are sold frozen or refrigerated. Egg roll skins may be substituted, although they have a different texture.

TIGER LILY BUDS. (Tiger lily stems, lily buds, golden needles, lily flowers or tiger lilies). Pale-gold dried lily buds are 2 to 3 inches long, with a delicate, musky flavor. Used as a vegetable or for flavoring, they must be soaked in water before using. They are sold in plastic bags and can be stored at room temperature.

TOFU. (Bean curd, dou fu, soybean curd or bean cake). Bland, smooth, custardlike mixture made from pureed soybeans. Tofu is fragile and requires little or no cooking. It is an inexpensive vegetable and a good source of protein. Refrigerate bean curd covered with water and tightly covered. Change water daily.

WATER CHESTNUTS. The crisp, white, delicately flavored bulb of an Asian marsh plant, the water chestnut is used as a vegetable for stir-frying and in soups and cold dishes. Fresh water chestnuts must be washed and peeled before using; canned, they are ready to eat. Pared jicama may be substituted.

WATER CHESTNUT FLOUR. The lumpy gray flour made from water chestnuts is used as a thickener or as an ingredient in light batters that fry to a crisp coating.

WHITE RADISH. (Icicle radish or daikon). These long white radishes, 6 to 12 inches long, are mild and sweet.

WINTER MELON. This round, green melon with translucent white pulp and yellow seeds is sold whole or in pieces by the pound.

WONTON SKINS. These thin, soft 3½-inch squares of dough are made from eggs, flour and water. They are filled with meat, vegetable or seafood mixtures, then deep-fried, boiled or steamed. The corners can be removed and the rounds used for dumplings. They are sold frozen or refrigerated. Egg roll skins, cut into quarters, may be substituted.

1

APPETIZERS AND
COLD DISHES

ALMOND CHICKEN

1 whole chicken breast (about 1 pound)
1 egg white
½ teaspoon salt
½ teaspoon sugar
⅛ teaspoon white pepper
¾ cup all-purpose flour
¾ cup water
2 tablespoons cornstarch
1 teaspoon salt
1 teaspoon baking soda
1 cup toasted slivered almonds
½ teaspoon almond extract
Vegetable oil
Plum Sweet-and-Sour Sauce (page 28)

Remove bones and skin from chicken breast; cut chicken into 1½-inch strips. Cut strips crosswise into ½-inch slices. Mix egg white, ½ teaspoon salt, the sugar and white pepper in medium bowl; stir in chicken. Cover and refrigerate 20 minutes.

Mix flour, water, cornstarch, 1 teaspoon salt, the baking soda, almonds and almond extract. Stir chicken into batter until well coated.

Heat vegetable oil (1½ inches) in wok to 350°. Fry chicken slices, about fifteen at a time, 2 to 3 minutes or until light brown, turning frequently; drain on paper towels. Increase oil temperature to 375°. Fry chicken all at one time about 1 minute or until golden brown; drain on paper towels. Serve with Plum Sweet-and-Sour Sauce.

About 20 appetizers

Clockwise from lower right: Almond Chicken, Pot Stickers (page 21), Barbecued Chicken Wings (page 16) and Pork Dumplings (page 22)

CHICKEN WING DRUMSTICKS

10 chicken wings
1 tablespoon cornstarch
1 teaspoon sugar
1 teaspoon salt
1 teaspoon light soy sauce
½ teaspoon five-spice powder
Vegetable oil
½ cup all-purpose flour
½ cup cold water
1 egg
3 tablespoons cornstarch
2 tablespoons vegetable oil
½ teaspoon baking soda
½ teaspoon salt

Cut each chicken wing at joint to make 2 pieces; reserve piece with tip to use in Chicken Broth (page 47). Cut skin and meat loose from narrow end of bone; push meat and skin down to large end of bone. Pull skin and meat down over end of bone to form a ball (see illustration). Mix 1 tablespoon cornstarch, the sugar, 1 teaspoon salt, the soy sauce and five-spice powder; sprinkle over chicken drumsticks. Cover and refrigerate 30 minutes.

Heat vegetable oil (1½ inches) in wok to 350°. Mix flour, water, egg, 3 tablespoons cornstarch, 2 tablespoons vegetable oil, the baking soda and ½ teaspoon salt. Dip ball end of each drumstick into batter. Fry 5 drumsticks at a time, 4 to 5 minutes or until light brown, turning 2 or 3 times; drain on paper towels.

Increase oil temperature to 375°. Fry drumsticks all at one time 2 minutes or until golden brown; drain on paper towels. Serve with Hot Mustard (page 28) and a sweet-and-sour sauce (pages 28–29) if desired.

10 drumsticks

The trimmed bones of these savory treats are convenient handles, turning chicken wings into practical finger food for buffets and cocktail parties. The uniquely Chinese five-spice powder makes these "lollipops" especially flavorful.

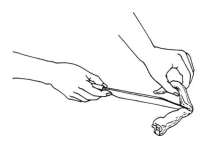

Cut each chicken wing at joint to make two pieces; discard piece with tip.

Cut skin and meat loose from narrow end of bone; push meat and skin down to large end of bone.

Chicken Wing Drumsticks

BARBECUED CHICKEN WINGS

12 chicken wings
¼ cup ketchup
1 tablespoon sugar
½ teaspoon salt
2 tablespoons finely chopped garlic
1 tablespoon vegetable oil
1 tablespoon Hoisin sauce
2 teaspoons soy sauce
1 teaspoon finely chopped gingerroot

Cut each chicken wing at joints to make 3 pieces; discard tip. Mix remaining ingredients in medium bowl; stir in chicken pieces until well coated. Cover and refrigerate 1 hour.

Heat oven to 450°. Place chicken with marinade in ungreased rectangular pan, 13 × 9 × 2 inches. Bake uncovered 30 minutes. Reduce oven temperature to 375°. Turn chicken; bake 20 minutes or until done and sauce is absorbed.

24 appetizers

COLD CHICKEN WITH HOT SAUCE

4 cups water
2 whole chicken breasts (about 2 pounds)
1 tablespoon sugar
2 tablespoons white wine vinegar
2 tablespoons soy sauce
2 tablespoons hot oil
1 teaspoon sesame oil
1 teaspoon finely chopped gingerroot
1 teaspoon finely chopped garlic
1 tablespoon chopped green onion (with top)

Heat water to boiling; add chicken. Heat to boiling; reduce heat to medium. Cover and simmer 10 minutes; remove from heat. Let stand covered 15 minutes; remove chicken from broth. Cool slightly; remove bones and skin from chicken. Cover and refrigerate chicken until cold.

Cut each chicken piece crosswise into ½-inch pieces. Place on serving platter.

Mix remaining ingredients except green onion until blended. Pour over chicken; sprinkle with green onion.

4 to 6 servings

陳 The chicken is removed from the heat and allowed to finish cooking in the hot broth as it stands. This method of cooking chicken, popular in Chinese cooking, results in chicken that is tender, juicy and never overcooked. Use the water in which the chicken is cooked as the base for chicken broth. Just add any bones, scraps of meat and wing tips you have been saving in the freezer. You may want to add a few slices of gingerroot. Simmer for 1 hour, then strain. Hot oil can be purchased at Oriental specialty stores. If you want to make your own, turn to Oil, Hot in the glossary for directions.

SESAME CHICKEN WINGS

12 chicken wings
1 egg
2 tablespoons vegetable oil
2 teaspoons soy sauce
1 teaspoon salt
1 teaspoon sugar
½ teaspoon white pepper
½ teaspoon five-spice powder
¼ cup cold water
½ cup all-purpose flour
¼ cup cornstarch
½ teaspoon baking soda
Vegetable oil
⅔ cup sugar
1 tablespoon cornstarch
½ cup vinegar
½ cup Chicken Broth (page 47)
2 teaspoons dark soy sauce
1 tablespoon vegetable oil
1 teaspoon red pepper sauce
1 teaspoon finely chopped garlic
2 tablespoons Toasted Sesame Seed (page 34)

Cut each chicken wing at joints to make 3 pieces; discard tip. Mix egg, 2 tablespoons vegetable oil, 2 teaspoons soy sauce, the salt, 1 teaspoon sugar, the white pepper and five-spice powder in medium bowl; stir in chicken. Cover and refrigerate 1 hour.

Stir water into chicken. Mix flour, ¼ cup cornstarch and the baking soda; stir into chicken.

Heat vegetable oil (2 inches) in wok to 350°. Fry 4 or 5 chicken pieces at a time, 3 minutes or until light brown, turning 2 or 3 times; drain on paper towels.

Increase oil temperature to 375°. Fry half of the chicken pieces 1 minute or until golden brown; drain on paper towels. Repeat with remaining pieces. Keep warm in 350° oven.

Mix ⅔ cup sugar and the cornstarch in 2-quart saucepan. Stir in vinegar, chicken broth, dark soy sauce, 1 tablespoon vegetable oil, the pepper sauce and garlic. Heat to boiling, stirring constantly, until mixture thickens.

Place chicken on heated serving platter. Pour sauce over; sprinkle with sesame seed.

24 appetizers

BARBECUED RIBS

2½- to 3-pound rack pork back ribs, cut
    across bones into halves
½ cup ketchup
2 tablespoons sugar
2 tablespoons Hoisin sauce
1 tablespoon dry white wine
2 teaspoons salt
2 large cloves garlic, finely chopped

Trim fat and remove membranes from ribs;
place ribs in shallow dish. Mix remaining ingredients. Pour mixture over ribs; turn ribs.
Cover and refrigerate at least 2 hours but no
longer than 24 hours.

Heat oven to 400°. Place ribs in single layer
on rack in roasting pan; brush with sauce.
Bake uncovered 30 minutes. Turn ribs; brush
with sauce. Bake uncovered until done, about
30 minutes longer. (Reduce oven temperature to 375° if ribs are thin.) Cut between
each rib to separate; serve with Hot Mustard
(page 28) if desired.

35 to 40 appetizers

BARBECUED PORK

3 pounds fresh pork tenderloins
½ cup ketchup
2 tablespoons sugar
2 tablespoons vegetable oil
1 tablespoon Hoisin sauce
1 tablespoon dry sherry or white wine
2 teaspoons salt
1 clove garlic, finely chopped

Place pork tenderloins in bowl. Mix remaining ingredients; pour over pork. Turn pork
to coat with marinade. Cover and refrigerate
at least 1 hour or up to 24 hours.

Heat oven to 450°. Place pork on rack or in
roasting pan. Bake uncovered 30 minutes.
Reduce oven temperature to 375°. Turn pork;
bake uncovered 20 minutes or until done.

Cool; cut pork on the diagonal into ¼-inch-
thick slices. Serve warm or cold with Hot Mustard (page 28) or a sweet-and-sour sauce (pages
28–29) if desired.

陳 *Barbecue more pork than you need and
freeze the surplus so you'll have it on hand
for spur-of-the-moment meals. For an authentic,
slightly charred taste, you should cook the pork over
a charcoal grill, but it will taste nearly as good
cooked in a conventional oven or on a rotisserie. If
using an oven, make sure it reaches 450° before
putting the pork in to roast; the high temperature
ensures juicy results. Barbecued Pork can be served
hot or cold. If you have made it ahead and want to
serve it hot, simply reheat in the microwave or
oven.*

Barbecued Ribs and Egg Rolls (page 26)

BARBECUED PORK BAO

1 tablespoon cornstarch
1 tablespoon cold water
2 tablespoons vegetable oil
2 cups chopped Barbecued Pork (page 18)
2 tablespoons oyster sauce
½ cup Chicken Broth (page 47)
1 cup milk
¼ cup sugar
1 tablespoon shortening
¼ teaspoon salt
1 package active dry yeast
2 tablespoons warm water (105 to 115°)
1 egg white
3 to 3 ½ cups all-purpose flour

Mix cornstarch and 1 tablespoon water.

Heat wok until very hot. Add vegetable oil; tilt wok to coat sides. Add Barbecued Pork; stir-fry 30 seconds. Stir in oyster sauce. Stir in broth; heat to boiling. Stir cornstarch mixture into pork mixture. Cook and stir about 10 seconds or until thickened. Cover and refrigerate.

Scald milk in 1-quart saucepan. Stir in sugar, shortening and salt until shortening is melted. Cool to lukewarm. Dissolve yeast in 2 tablespoons water. Stir yeast and egg white into milk mixture. Pour milk mixture over 3¼ cups of the flour in medium bowl; stir until smooth. Mix in enough remaining flour to make a stiff dough that is easy to handle.

Turn dough onto lightly floured surface; knead about 4 minutes or until smooth and elastic. Place in greased bowl; turn greased side up. Cover; let rise in warm place 1 to 1½ hours or until double. (Dough is ready if indentation remains when touched.)

Punch down dough; divide into 20 pieces. Roll or pat each piece into 3½-inch circle. Place 1 tablespoon pork mixture in center of circle. Bring edge up around filling; twist to seal (see illustration). Place on 3-inch square of waxed paper. Repeat with remaining circles. Cover; let rise in warm place 30 minutes. Place 5 or 6 bao ½ inch apart on heatproof plate on rack in steamer; cover and steam over boiling water 12 minutes. Repeat with remaining bao. (Add boiling water if necessary.) Remove waxed paper squares immediately.

20 bao

Bring edge up around filling; twist to seal.

Serve these filled yeast rolls for breakfast or lunch as well as for appetizers, or for an after-school snack as they do in China. Bao are convenient for picnics too, because they can be wrapped in foil and "steamed" over a grill or even an open fire. You can make, cover and refrigerate them up to 2 days ahead, or freeze as long as 2 months. Steam refrigerated bao 5 minutes, frozen bao for 30.

POT STICKERS

4 medium dried black mushrooms

1 pound lean ground pork

⅓ cup finely chopped canned bamboo shoots

¼ cup finely chopped green onions (with tops)

1 tablespoon dry white wine

1 tablespoon water

1 teaspoon cornstarch

1 teaspoon salt

1 teaspoon sesame oil

Dash of white pepper

2 cups all-purpose flour

1 cup boiling water

½ cup vegetable oil

2 cups water

2 tablespoons soy sauce

1 teaspoon sesame oil

Soak mushrooms in hot water 20 minutes or until soft, drain. Rinse in warm water; drain. Squeeze out excess moisture. Remove and discard stems; chop caps finely. Mix mushrooms, pork, bamboo shoots, green onions, wine, 1 tablespoon water, the cornstarch, salt, 1 teaspoon sesame oil and the white pepper.

Mix flour and 1 cup boiling water until a soft dough forms. Knead dough on lightly floured surface about 5 minutes or until smooth. Divide dough into halves. Shape each half into roll 12 inches long; cut each roll into ½-inch slices. Roll 1 slice of dough into a 3-inch circle. Place 1 tablespoon pork mixture on center of circle. Pinch 5 pleats on edge of one half of circle. Fold circle in half, pressing pleated edge to unpleated edge (see illustration). Repeat with remaining slices of dough.

Heat wok until very hot. Add 2 tablespoons of the vegetable oil; tilt wok to coat side. Place dumplings in single layer in wok; fry 2 minutes or until bottoms are golden brown. Add ½ cup of the water. Cover and cook 6 to 7

minutes or until water is absorbed. Repeat with remaining dumplings. (Add vegetable oil as necessary.) Mix soy sauce and 1 teaspoon sesame oil; serve with dumplings.

48 dumplings

Place pork mixture on center of circle. Pinch five pleats on edge of one half of circle.

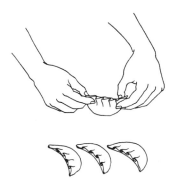

Fold circle in half, pressing pleated edge to unpleated edge.

Pot Stickers are sometimes misunderstood by Westerners. One uninitiated diner was overheard to tell his companion in a restaurant buffet line, "Don't take those, they're burned on the bottom." Well, they're supposed to be that way—crisply browned on the bottom with floppy, soft, steamed tops. Getting them to stick just the right amount may take some practice; don't get discouraged if the first few tear when you try to get them out of the wok, they'll taste great anyway.

SICHUAN CHICKEN DUMPLINGS

½ pound cabbage

⅛ teaspoon salt

2 green onions (with tops)

⅓ cup ketchup

¼ cup Hoisin sauce

2 teaspoons chili paste

1 tablespoon soy sauce

½ pound boneless skinless chicken thighs

1 green onion (with top), finely chopped

½ teaspoon sugar

½ teaspoon finely chopped gingerroot

½ egg white

½ teaspoon salt

1 tablespoon cornstarch

25 to 30 siu mai skins* (about ¾ pound)

2 quarts water

2 tablespoons vegetable oil

Place cabbage in workbowl of food processor fitted with steel blade. Cover and process until finely chopped. Sprinkle ⅛ teaspoon salt over cabbage in medium bowl; let stand at room temperature 30 minutes. Squeeze out excess water. Cut 2 green onions diagonally into 2-inch pieces. Mix ketchup, Hoisin sauce, chili paste and soy sauce.

Place chicken thighs in workbowl of food processor fitted with steel blade. Cover and process until finely chopped. Combine chicken, cabbage, chopped green onions, sugar, gingerroot, egg white, ½ teaspoon salt and the cornstarch in medium bowl.

Hold siu mai skin in hand. (Cover remaining skins with plastic wrap to keep them pliable.) Wet the edge of half of the circle closest to fingers. Pinch 2 or 3 pleats into the wet edge. Place 1 heaping teaspoon chicken mixture in center of skin. Fold circle in half, pressing pleated edge to unpleated edge to seal dump-

ling (see illustration page 21). Repeat with remaining skins. (Cover filled dumplings with plastic wrap to keep them from drying out.)

Heat water to boiling in Dutch oven; add dumplings. Heat to boiling; reduce heat. Simmer uncovered 2 minutes; drain. Immediately rinse dumplings in cold water; cover with iced water to prevent them from sticking together.

Heat vegetable oil in 12-inch skillet over high heat. Add ketchup mixture; heat to boiling, stirring constantly. Add dumplings; cook uncovered 3 minutes. Stir in green onion pieces.

25 to 30 appetizers

*Wonton skins can be substituted for siu mai skins. Cut off corners to make a circle.

PORK DUMPLINGS

8 medium dried black mushrooms

1 pound lean ground pork

½ cup finely chopped canned bamboo shoots

¼ cup finely chopped green onions (with tops)

1 egg white

2 tablespoons cornstarch

2 teaspoons salt

2 teaspoons light soy sauce

½ teaspoon sesame oil

¼ teaspoon white pepper

40 siu mai skins* (about 1 pound)

¼ cup light soy sauce

⅛ teaspoon sesame oil

Soak mushrooms in hot water 20 minutes or until soft; drain. Rinse in warm water; drain. Squeeze out excess moisture. Remove and discard stems; chop caps finely. Mix mushrooms, pork, bamboo shoots, green onions, egg white, cornstarch, salt, 2 teaspoons soy sauce, ½ teaspoon sesame oil and the white pepper.

Hold siu mai skin in hand. (Cover remaining skins with plastic wrap to keep them pliable.) Place 1 tablespoon pork mixture in center of skin. Bring edge of skin up side of filling, leaving top open. Repeat with remaining skins. (Cover filled dumplings with plastic wrap to keep them from drying out.)

Place dumplings in single layer on rack in steamer; cover and steam over boiling water 20 minutes. (Add boiling water if necessary.) Repeat with remaining dumplings. Mix ¼ cup soy sauce and ⅛ teaspoon sesame oil; serve with dumplings.

40 dumplings

*Wonton skins can be substituted for siu mai skins. Cut off corners to make a circle.

CRABMEAT PUFFS

1 package (6 ounces) frozen crabmeat, thawed
2 packages (3 ounces each) cream cheese, softened
½ teaspoon salt
¼ teaspoon garlic powder
40 wonton skins (about 1 pound)
1 egg, slightly beaten
Vegetable oil

Drain crabmeat thoroughly; remove cartilage. Remove excess water by squeezing crabmeat; chop.

Mix crabmeat, cream cheese, salt and garlic powder.

Brush wonton skin with egg. Place heaping teaspoonful crabmeat mixture in center of wonton skin. (Cover remaining skins with plastic wrap to keep them pliable.) Top with another wonton skin; press edges to seal. Brush egg on center of each side of puff. Make a pleat on each of 4 sides, pressing to seal (see

illustration). Repeat with remaining wonton skins. (Cover puffs with plastic wrap to keep them from drying out.)

Heat vegetable oil (1½ inches) in wok to 350°. Fry 4 or 5 puffs at a time, 2 minutes or until golden brown, turning 2 or 3 times; drain on paper towels. Serve with a sweet-and-sour sauce (pages 28–29) if desired.

20 appetizers

Place crabmeat mixture in center of wonton skin; top with another wonton skin and press edges to seal.

Brush egg on center of each side of puff; make a pleat on each side, pressing to seal.

STIR-FRIED WONTONS WITH SICHUAN SAUCE

¼ pound raw medium shrimp (in shells)

2 ounces lean ground pork

3 whole water chestnuts, finely chopped

2 green onions (with tops), chopped

1 teaspoon cornstarch

½ teaspoon salt

¼ teaspoon sesame oil

Dash of white pepper

⅓ cup ketchup

¼ cup Hoisin sauce

2 teaspoons chili paste

1 tablespoon soy sauce

24 wonton skins (about ½ pound)

1 egg white, slightly beaten

5 cups water

2 tablespoons vegetable oil

Peel shrimp. Make a shallow cut lengthwise down back of each shrimp; wash out vein. Chop shrimp finely. Mix shrimp, pork, water chestnuts, green onions, cornstarch, salt, sesame oil and white pepper. Mix ketchup, Hoisin sauce, chili paste and soy sauce.

Place ½ teaspoon shrimp mixture in center of wonton skin. (Cover remaining skins with plastic wrap to keep them pliable.) Fold bottom corner of wonton skin over filling to opposite corner, forming a triangle. Brush right corner of triangle with egg white. Bring corners together below filling; pinch left corner to right corner to seal (see illustration). Repeat with remaining wonton skins. (Cover filled wontons with plastic wrap to keep them from drying out.)

Heat water to boiling in Dutch oven; add wontons. Heat to boiling; reduce heat. Simmer uncovered 2 minutes; drain. Immediately rinse wontons in cold water; cover with iced water to keep them from sticking together.

Heat vegetable oil in 12-inch skillet, over high heat; add ketchup mixture. Heat to boiling, stirring constantly. Add wontons; cook uncovered 3 minutes.

24 appetizers

Fried Wontons: Fill wontons as directed above except omit cooking in water and ketchup mixture. Heat oil (1½ inches) in wok to 350°. Fry 8 to 10 wontons at a time, turning 2 or 3 times, 3 minutes until golden brown. Drain on paper towels. Serve with Hot Mustard (page 28) or a sweet-and-sour sauce (pages 28–29).

Fold bottom corner of wonton skin over filling to opposite corner, forming a triangle.

Brush one corner of triangle with egg white; bring corners together and press to seal.

Stir-fried Wontons with Sichuan Sauce

EGG ROLLS

4 or 5 medium dried black mushrooms
½ pound lean ground pork
½ teaspoon salt
½ teaspoon cornstarch
½ teaspoon soy sauce
Dash of white pepper
8 cups water
1 head green cabbage (about 2½ pounds),
    finely shredded
2 tablespoons vegetable oil
¼ cup shredded canned bamboo shoots
½ pound cooked and cleaned shrimp, finely
    chopped
⅓ cup fine chopped green onions (with tops)
1 teaspoon salt
1 teaspoon five-spice powder
18 egg roll skins (about 1 pound)
1 egg, beaten
Vegetable oil

Soak mushrooms in hot water 20 minutes or until soft; drain. Rinse in warm water; drain. Squeeze out excess moisture. Remove and discard stems; cut caps into thin strips. Mix pork, ½ teaspoon salt, the cornstarch, soy sauce and white pepper. Cover and refrigerate about 20 minutes.

Heat water to boiling in Dutch oven; add cabbage. Heat to boiling; cover and cook 1 minute. Drain; rinse cabbage with cold water until cold. Drain thoroughly; remove excess water by squeezing cabbage.

Heat wok until very hot. Add 2 tablespoons vegetable oil; tilt wok to coat sides. Add pork; stir-fry 2 minutes or until pork is no longer pink. Add mushrooms and bamboo shoots; stir-fry 1 minute. Stir in cabbage, shrimp, green onions, 1 teaspoon salt and the five-spice powder. Remove cabbage mixture from wok; cool.

Place ½ cup cabbage mixture slightly below center of egg roll skin. (Cover remaining skins with plastic wrap to keep them pliable.) Fold corner of egg roll skin closest to filling over filling, tucking the point under (see illustration). Fold in and overlap the two opposite corners. Brush fourth corner with egg; roll up to seal. Repeat with remaining egg roll skins. (Cover filled egg rolls with plastic wrap to keep them from drying out.)

Heat vegetable oil (2 inches) in wok to 350°. Fry 4 or 5 egg rolls at a time 2 to 3 minutes or until golden brown, turning 2 or 3 times; drain on paper towels. Serve with Hot Mustard (page 28) and a sweet-and-sour sauce (pages 28–29) if desired.

16 to 18 egg rolls

Fold corner over filling; tuck point under filling.

Fold in and overlap the two opposite corners. Brush remaining corner with egg; roll up to seal.

CHILLED SPRING ROLLS

5 eggs
Dash of salt
Dash of white pepper
2½ teaspoons vegetable oil
2 green onions (with tops)
10 ounces bean sprouts
10 leaf lettuce leaves
10 imitation whole crab legs, each 2 inches
    long
1 teaspoon sesame oil
1 package ready-to-eat spring roll skins
Honey Sichuan Sauce (right)

Beat eggs, salt and white pepper. Heat 8-inch skillet over medium heat until hot. Add ½ teaspoon vegetable oil; tilt skillet to coat bottom. Add ¼ cup egg mixture; immediately tilt skillet until egg covers the bottom forming a thin pancake. Cook about 1 minute or until firm; turn and cook about 10 seconds or just until dry. Wipe out skillet; repeat 4 more times. Cover and refrigerate fried eggs until cold.

Cut green onions into 2-inch pieces. Cut pieces lengthwise into thin strips. Mix green onions and bean sprouts; divide mixture into 10 equal parts. Tear each lettuce leaf into a 3-inch square. Sprinkle crab legs with sesame oil. Cut each fried egg into halves.

Place one lettuce square in center of spring roll skin; top with one fried egg half. (Cover remaining skins with plastic wrap to keep them pliable.) Place one part bean sprout mixture on egg; top with one crab leg. Fold bottom corner of spring roll skin over filling, tucking the point under. Fold in and overlap the two opposite corners. Brush fourth corner generously with cold water; roll up to seal. Repeat with remaining spring roll skins. (Cover filled spring rolls with plastic wrap to keep them from drying out.) Cover and refrigerate 2 hours but no longer than 8 hours. Cut into halves; serve with Honey Sichuan Sauce.

20 appetizers.

Honey Sichuan Sauce

½ cup honey
½ cup chili paste

Mix ingredients.

CRISPY SCALLOPS

1 pound sea scallops
½ teaspoon salt
¼ teaspoon white pepper
1 teaspoon sesame oil
1 egg white
1 tablespoon cornstarch
Vegetable oil
½ cup water
½ cup all-purpose flour
¼ cup cornstarch
1 tablespoon vegetable oil
½ teaspoon baking soda
½ teaspoon salt

Rinse scallops in cold water 3 or 4 times; drain thoroughly. Pat scallops dry with paper towel. Mix ½ teaspoon salt, the white pepper, sesame oil, egg white and 1 tablespoon cornstarch in medium bowl; stir in scallops. Cover and refrigerate 30 minutes.

Heat vegetable oil (1½ inches) in wok to 350°. Mix water, flour, ¼ cup cornstarch, 1 tablespoon vegetable oil, the baking soda and ½ teaspoon salt in medium bowl. Stir scallops into batter until well coated. Fry 8 scallops at a time 2 minutes or until light brown, turning occasionally; drain on paper towels.

Increase oil temperature to 375°. Fry scallops all at one time about 1 minute or until golden brown; drain on paper towels.

Serve with Hot Mustard (page 28) and a sweet-and-sour sauce (pages 28–29) if desired.

About 25 appetizers

SHRIMP TOAST

½ pound raw medium shrimp (in shells)
½ cup chopped green onions (with tops)
¼ cup all-purpose flour
¼ cup water
1 egg
1 tablespoon cornstarch
1 teaspoon salt
¼ teaspoon sugar
¼ teaspoon sesame oil
Dash of white pepper
Vegetable oil
5 slices white bread

Peel shrimp. Make a shallow cut lengthwise down back of each shrimp; wash out vein. Cut shrimp lengthwise into halves; cut each half crosswise into halves. Pat shrimp dry with paper towels.

Mix shrimp, green onions, flour, water, egg, cornstarch, salt, sugar, sesame oil and white pepper.

Heat vegetable oil (1½ inches) in wok to 350°. Remove crusts from bread; cut each slice into 4 squares. Place 1 or 2 pieces shrimp with sauce on each bread square.

Fry 5 squares at a time, about 2 minutes or until golden brown, turning frequently; drain on paper towels.

20 appetizers

For this deep-fried appetizer that seems to defy gravity, spread shrimp onto bite-size bread squares for an irresistible addition to a cocktail buffet, or serve them as an impressive first course for a Chinese feast or an elegant dinner of any nationality. Shrimp Toast can be cooked up to 3 hours ahead. Reheat in a preheated 425° oven for 5 minutes.

HOT MUSTARD

¼ cup dry mustard
3 tablespoons plus 1½ teaspoons cold water

Mix mustard and water until smooth. Let stand 5 minutes before serving. Cover and refrigerate any remaining mustard. Serve with appetizers.

⅓ cup

PLUM SWEET-AND-SOUR SAUCE

1 can (20 ounces) crushed pineapple in heavy
    syrup
1 cup sugar
1 cup water
1 cup vinegar
1 tablespoon dark soy sauce
2 tablespoons cornstarch
2 tablespoons cold water
1 cup plum sauce or plum jam*

Heat pineapple (with syrup), sugar, 1 cup water, the vinegar and soy sauce to boiling. Mix cornstarch and 2 tablespoons water; stir into pineapple mixture. Heat to boiling, stirring constantly. Cool to room temperature; stir in plum sauce. Cover and refrigerate. Serve with appetizers.

5⅔ cups

*Orange marmalade can be substituted for the plum sauce.

RED SWEET-AND-SOUR SAUCE

½ cup red wine vinegar
½ cup ketchup
⅓ cup sugar
15 drops red pepper sauce

Mix all ingredients. Cover and refrigerate. Serve with appetizers.

1¼ cups

CRABMEAT SALAD

¼ cup water
¼ cup white vinegar
¼ cup sugar
½ teaspoon salt
2 teaspoons finely chopped garlic
1 tablespoon sesame oil
Vegetable oil
2 ounces rice stick noodles
½ head iceberg lettuce, shredded (about 3 cups)
6 ounces cooked crabmeat
2 tablespoons chopped green onions (with tops)
1 tablespoon Toasted Sesame Seed (page 34)

Heat water, vinegar, sugar and salt to boiling over medium-high heat. Cook uncovered 5 minutes; cool. Stir in garlic and sesame oil. Cover and refrigerate dressing.

Heat vegetable oil (1 inch) in wok to 425°. Pull noodles apart. Fry the noodles, ¼ at a time, about 5 seconds or until puffed, turning once, drain on paper towels.

Toss lettuce and crabmeat with dressing until evenly coated. Let stand 5 minutes; drain. Add rice noodles, green onions and sesame seed; toss.

4 servings

CHICKEN-PINEAPPLE SALAD

2 whole chicken breasts (about 2 pounds)
½ teaspoon salt
⅛ teaspoon white pepper
1 teaspoon cornstarch
3 tablespoons vegetable oil
1 teaspoon finely chopped gingerroot
1 cup Plum Sweet-and-Sour Sauce (page 28)
1 medium green bell pepper
1 medium red bell pepper
1½ cups pineapple chunks
1 cup skinless raw peanuts, if desired

Remove bones and skin from chicken breasts; cut chicken crosswise into ¼-inch slices. Toss chicken, salt and white pepper in medium bowl. Cover and refrigerate 20 minutes. Sprinkle cornstarch evenly over chicken; toss to coat chicken evenly.

Heat wok until very hot. Add vegetable oil; tilt wok to coat side. Add chicken and gingerroot; stir-fry until chicken turns white. Reduce heat to medium; cook and stir 2 minutes. Remove chicken from wok; cover and refrigerate until cold. Prepare Plum Sweet-and-Sour Sauce.

Cut bell peppers into 1-inch pieces. Toss chicken, bell peppers, pineapple and peanuts. Add sweet-and-sour sauce; toss until evenly coated.

4 servings

🈺 *For an elegant luncheon presentation, use fresh pineapple and serve the salad in hollowed, quartered pineapple shells.*

CHINESE CHICKEN SALAD

Vegetable oil
2 ounces cellophane noodles (bean threads)
2 cups shredded cooked chicken
½ head iceberg lettuce, shredded (about
    3 cups)
1 small carrot, shredded (about ½ cup)
½ cup canned shoestring potatoes
1 tablespoon Toasted Sesame Seed (page 34)
⅓ cup mayonnaise or salad dressing
1 tablespoon sugar
2 tablespoons white wine vinegar
2 tablespoons Hoisin sauce
1 tablespoon sesame oil
1 teaspoon light soy sauce
1 tablespoon chopped green onion (with top)

Heat vegetable oil (1 inch) in wok to 425°. Fry the noodles, ¼ at a time, about 5 seconds or until puffed, turning once; drain on paper towels. Wash and thoroughly dry wok.

Place ½ of the noodles, the chicken, lettuce, carrot and shoestring potatoes in large bowl; sprinkle with sesame seed.

Mix mayonnaise, sugar, vinegar, Hoisin sauce, sesame oil and soy sauce. Pour sauce over chicken and vegetables; top with remaining noodles and green onion. Toss before serving.

4 to 6 servings

CHICKEN-PAPAYA SALAD

4 cups water
2 whole chicken breasts (about 2 pounds)
Gingered Pineapple Dressing (page 33)
4 ounces Chinese pea pods
1 large papaya
1 small green onion (with top), chopped
Lettuce leaves

Heat water to boiling; add chicken. Heat to boiling; reduce heat to medium. Cover and simmer 10 minutes; remove from heat. Let stand covered 15 minutes; remove chicken from broth. Cool slightly; remove bones and skin from chicken. Cover and refrigerate chicken until cold.

Cut chicken into 1-inch pieces. Prepare Gingered Pineapple Dressing. Toss chicken and half of the dressing. Let stand 10 minutes.

Remove strings from pea pods. Place pea pods in boiling water; heat to boiling. Immediately rinse in cold water; drain. Cut pea pods into halves. Pare papaya; cut into ¾-inch pieces. Toss chicken mixture, pea pods, papaya, green onion and remaining dressing until evenly coated. Arrange lettuce leaves on serving platter. Spoon chicken mixture on lettuce; garnish with diced pimiento or red bell pepper if desired.

4 servings

You may substitute cantaloupe for the papaya if you like a slightly less sweet salad. You'll need about 4 cups of ¾-inch melon pieces, approximately 1 large melon. As a refreshing first course or side dish, this salad will serve 8; it makes a light lunch for 4.

Lotus Root Salad (page 34) and Chicken-Papaya Salad

PINEAPPLE SALAD WITH BARBECUED PORK

Barbecued Pork (page 18)
Gingered Pineapple Dressing (below)
½ pineapple
4 ounces jicama
½ medium red bell pepper
1 small green onion (with top)
Lettuce leaves

Prepare Barbecued Pork; cover and refrigerate. Prepare Gingered Pineapple Dressing. Pare pineapple; remove core. Cut pineapple into fourths; cut each fourth into very thin slices. Pare jicama; cut into 1-inch-wide pieces. Cut pieces into very thin slices. Place pineapple and jicama in glass or plastic bowl. Add Gingered Pineapple Dressing; toss gently. Cover and refrigerate up to 12 hours.

Cut pork diagonally into ¼-inch slices. Cut bell pepper into ½-inch pieces. Cut green onion diagonally into ⅛-inch slices. Arrange lettuce leaves on serving platter. Arrange pork and pineapple mixture on lettuce. Sprinkle with bell pepper and green onion.

4 servings

Gingered Pineapple Dressing

½ cup mayonnaise or salad dressing
¼ cup pineapple preserves
2 tablespoons lemon juice
1 teaspoon sugar
1 teaspoon gingerroot juice (page 9)
1 teaspoon sesame oil

Mix all ingredients.

MARINATED BROCCOLI

3 cups bite-size broccoli flowerets
⅓ cup mayonnaise or salad dressing
1 tablespoon sugar
2 tablespoons white wine vinegar
2 tablespoons Hoisin sauce
1 tablespoon sesame oil
1 teaspoon light soy sauce
1 teaspoon chili paste

Place broccoli in boiling water; heat to boiling. Boil uncovered 1 minute; drain. Immediately rinse in cold water; drain. Mix remaining ingredients; stir in broccoli. Cover and refrigerate 1 hour. Drain just before serving.

4 servings

LOTUS ROOT SALAD

10 ounces lotus root*
1 medium red bell pepper
½ medium green bell pepper
½ hot green chili
¼ cup red wine vinegar
2 tablespoons sugar
2 tablespoons light soy sauce
3 tablespoons sesame oil
1 tablespoon Toasted Sesame Seed (right)

Pare lotus root; cut crosswise into thin slices. Cut bell peppers into ¼-inch strips. Remove seeds and membrane from chili. Cut chili into very thin slices. Mix vinegar, sugar and soy sauce. Stir in sesame oil. Toss lotus root, bell pepper, chili and dressing. Cover and refrigerate 1 hour.

Toss salad just before serving; sprinkle with sesame seed.

6 servings

Lotus roots are symbolic: The Chinese words for lotus root and the expression that means "achieve more each year" sound almost identical and so lotus root has become a traditional New Year's food. This vegetable can be used in salads, stir-fries and stews or soups. Thinly sliced, a little goes a long way.

*You can substitute ½ can (16-ounce size) sliced lotus root, drained, for the fresh lotus root.

BEAN SPROUT SALAD

16 ounces bean sprouts
2 green onions (with tops)
½ medium red bell pepper
1 tablespoon sugar
2 tablespoons Hoisin sauce
2 tablespoons white wine vinegar
2 teaspoons sesame oil
2 teaspoons light soy sauce
2 tablespoons vegetable oil
1 teaspoon finely chopped garlic
1 teaspoon salt
2 tablespoons Toasted Sesame Seed (below)

Rinse bean sprouts under cold water; drain. Cut green onions into 2-inch pieces; shred lengthwise into fine strips. Cut bell pepper into thin strips. Mix sugar, Hoisin sauce, vinegar, sesame oil and soy sauce.

Heat wok until very hot. Add vegetable oil; tilt wok to coat side. Add garlic, salt and bean sprouts; stir-fry 2 minutes. Remove bean sprouts from wok; drain and cool. Toss beans sprouts, green onions, bell pepper and dressing; sprinkle with sesame seed.

4 servings

Toasted Sesame Seed

1 tablespoon sesame seed

Heat 8-inch skillet until hot; reduce heat to medium low. Add sesame seed; cook and stir until sesame seed are light brown, about 2 minutes.

SPINACH WITH PLUM SAUCE DRESSING

16 ounces spinach, torn into pieces
    (about 6 cups)
4 ounces cooked and cleaned shrimp
2 tablespoons diced red bell pepper or
    pimiento
8 small mushrooms, sliced
Plum Sauce Dressing (below)
¼ cup toasted slivered almonds

Toss spinach, shrimp, bell pepper, mushrooms
and Plum Sauce Dressing until spinach is
evenly coated. Sprinkle with almonds.

6 servings

Plum Sauce Dressing

½ cup Plum Sweet-and-Sour Sauce
    (page 28)
2 tablespoons vegetable oil
2 tablespoons frozen (thawed) orange juice
    concentrate
1½ teaspoons dried red pepper flakes
1 tablespoon finely chopped garlic

Mix all ingredients with wire whisk or fork
until blended.

MARINATED MUSHROOMS AND CUCUMBERS

1 medium cucumber
1 teaspoon salt
8 ounces small mushrooms
1 tablespoon vegetable oil
¼ cup white wine vinegar
2 tablespoons sugar
1 tablespoon light soy sauce
1 tablespoon chili paste
1 tablespoon sesame oil

Pare cucumber; cut lengthwise into halves and
remove seeds. Cut cucumber diagonally into
½-inch slices. Sprinkle salt over cucumber in
small bowl. Let stand at room temperature 30
minutes. Squeeze out excess moisture; pat cucumber dry with paper towels. Cut mushrooms into halves; toss with vegetable oil.

Mix vinegar, sugar, soy sauce, chili paste and
sesame oil; toss with cucumber and mushrooms. Cover and refrigerate 1 hour, stirring
1 or 2 times. Drain just before serving. Garnish with chopped green onion if desired.

4 servings

2

湯

SOUPS

SHRIMP-TOFU BALL SOUP

12 Chinese pea pods
6 ounces firm tofu
½ pound raw medium shrimp (in shells)
1 egg white
1 tablespoon cornstarch
⅛ teaspoon white pepper
1 teaspoon sesame oil
1 teaspoon vegetable oil
1 teaspoon salt
4 cups Chicken Broth (page 47)
1 teaspoon salt
1 green onion (with top), chopped

Remove strings from pea pods; cut pea pods diagonally into halves. Rinse tofu under cold water; drain. Mash tofu with a fork.

Peel shrimp. Make a shallow cut lengthwise down back of each shrimp; wash out vein.

Chop shrimp finely. Mix shrimp, tofu, egg white, cornstarch, white pepper, sesame oil, vegetable oil and 1 teaspoon salt. Shape shrimp mixture into 1-inch balls.

Heat broth and 1 teaspoon salt to boiling in 2-quart saucepan. Add shrimp balls to broth; heat to boiling. Add pea pods; boil 1 minute. Remove from heat; stir in green onion.

4 or 5 servings

Tofu *is the Japanese name for bean curd, a wonderful source of cholesterol-free protein. In itself mild in flavor, tofu readily absorbs the tastes of any ingredients with which it is cooked. It is very perishable and should be kept submerged in water in your refrigerator. You can keep it for a couple of days if you change the water daily. The shrimp balls in this soup are rather delicate so you may want to use a spoon to place them gently in the broth.*

RED SNAPPER AND CELERY CABBAGE SOUP

½ pound skinless red snapper or sea bass
  fillets
1 teaspoon cornstarch
1 teaspoon finely chopped gingerroot
1 teaspoon vegetable oil
1 teaspoon sesame oil
½ teaspoon salt
½ teaspoon light soy sauce
⅛ teaspoon white pepper
8 ounces celery cabbage
4 cups Chicken Broth (page 47)
1 teaspoon salt
1 teaspoon sesame oil
2 tablespoons chopped green onions (with
  tops)

Cut fish fillets crosswise into ½-inch slices. Toss fish, cornstarch, gingerroot, vegetable oil, 1 teaspoon sesame oil, ½ teaspoon salt, the soy sauce and white pepper in medium bowl. Cover and refrigerate 30 minutes. Cut celery cabbage into ½-inch slices.

Heat broth and 1 teaspoon salt to boiling in 3-quart saucepan. Add celery cabbage; heat to boiling. Stir in fish; heat to boiling. Reduce heat to medium, simmer uncovered 2 minutes. Remove from heat; stir in 1 teaspoon sesame oil and green onions.

4 or 5 servings

Celery cabbage, also known as Chinese cabbage, cooks in minutes and adds a unique, authentic flavor to this light and spicy soup. Use a firm fish such as red snapper, sea bass, walleye or flounder and be sure not to overcook, or the fish will break into tiny bits. Be careful when ladling the soup into the serving bowls, for the same reason.

WINTER MELON SOUP

6 medium dried black mushrooms
1 whole chicken breast (about 1 pound)
½ teaspoon cornstarch
½ teaspoon salt
1 pound winter melon
¼ pound fully cooked smoked ham
½ cup sliced canned bamboo shoots
4 cups Chicken Broth (page 47)
1 teaspoon salt
⅛ teaspoon white pepper

Soak mushrooms in hot water about 20 minutes or until soft; drain. Rinse in warm water; drain. Squeeze out excess moisture. Remove and discard stems; cut caps into ¼-inch pieces.

Remove bones and skin from chicken; cut chicken into ½-inch pieces. Toss chicken, cornstarch and ½ teaspoon salt in medium bowl. Cover and refrigerate 20 minutes.

Remove rind, seeds and fibers from melon. Cut melon into ½-inch pieces. Cut ham and bamboo shoots into ½-inch pieces.

Heat broth to boiling in 3-quart saucepan. Add mushrooms, melon and bamboo shoots; heat to boiling. Stir in chicken and ham. Heat to boiling; reduce heat. Cover and simmer 10 minutes. Stir in 1 teaspoon salt and the white pepper.

6 servings

PEANUT SOUP

7 cups water
¾ cup skinless raw peanuts
6 medium dried black mushrooms
½ medium onion
2 small tomatoes
1 tablespoon vegetable oil
1 teaspoon salt
1 teaspoon sugar

Heat water to boiling; reduce heat. Add peanuts; cover and simmer 1½ hours. (Do not boil or broth will be cloudy.)

Soak mushrooms in hot water 20 minutes or until soft; drain. Rinse in warm water; drain. Squeeze out excess moisture. Remove and discard stems; cut caps into ½-inch pieces. Cut onion into ½-inch pieces. Place tomatoes in boiling water; boil 1 minute. Immediately place in cold water. Remove peel and seeds; cut into ½-inch pieces.

Heat wok until very hot. Add vegetable oil; tilt wok to coat side. Add onion; stir-fry until crisp-tender. Add mushrooms and tomatoes; stir-fry 2 minutes. Stir in salt and sugar. Add vegetable mixture to peanuts and broth. Heat to boiling; reduce heat. Simmer covered 20 minutes.

6 servings

 Raw peanuts can be found in health food stores and Oriental groceries.

TOMATO EGG DROP SOUP

6 dried black mushrooms
1 large tomato
4 cups Chicken Broth (page 47)
1 tablespoon vegetable oil
1 small onion, sliced
2 eggs
1 teaspoon salt
½ teaspoon white pepper

Soak mushrooms in hot water 20 minutes or until soft; drain. Rinse in warm water; drain. Squeeze out excess moisture. Remove and discard stems; cut caps into thin strips. Place tomato in boiling water; boil 10 seconds. Immediately place in cold water. Peel; cut into 8 wedges; cut each wedge into halves.

Heat broth to boiling in 3-quart saucepan. Heat wok until hot. Add vegetable oil; tilt wok to coat side. Add onion; stir-fry 1 minute. Add mushrooms and tomato; stir-fry 2 minutes.

Stir tomato mixture into broth; reduce heat to medium. Cover and simmer 5 minutes. Heat to rolling boil over high heat. (If broth is not heated to a rolling boil, egg will not form threads.)

Mix eggs, salt and pepper. Pour egg mixture slowly into broth, stirring constantly with fork, until egg forms threads.

4 or 5 servings

 Stir-fried onion, tomato and black mushrooms add color, texture and flavor to classic egg drop soup. Garnish with sprigs of cilantro; it complements the tomato flavor exquisitely.

EGG DROP SOUP

3 cups Chicken Broth (page 47)
1 teaspoon salt
Dash of white pepper
1 medium green onion (with top), chopped
2 eggs, slightly beaten

Heat broth, salt and white pepper to rolling boil in 2-quart saucepan over high heat. (If broth is not heated to a rolling boil, egg will not form threads.)

Stir green onion into eggs. Pour egg mixture slowly into broth, stirring constantly with fork, until egg forms threads.

3 servings

This is a Chinese standard and among the simplest soups in the world to make. The only trick is to be sure the broth is at a full, rolling boil as you stir in the beaten eggs. This ensures that the soup's signature thin threads of cooked egg float throughout.

BEEF EGG DROP SOUP

6 ounces beef boneless sirloin or
     flank steak
½ teaspoon cornstarch
¼ teaspoon salt
⅛ teaspoon white pepper
2 tablespoons cornstarch
2 tablespoons water
2 eggs
½ teaspoon salt
4 cups beef broth
4 thin slices peeled gingerroot
½ teaspoon salt
1 tablespoon chopped green onion (with top)

Trim fat from beef steak; cut beef lengthwise into 2-inch strips. Cut strips crosswise into ⅛-inch slices. Toss beef, ½ teaspoon cornstarch, ¼ teaspoon salt and the white pepper in medium bowl. Cover and refrigerate 20 minutes.

Mix 2 tablespoons cornstarch and water. Beat eggs and ½ teaspoon salt.

Heat broth to boiling in 3-quart saucepan. Add gingerroot and ½ teaspoon salt; boil 2 minutes. Add beef; stir to separate pieces. Heat to boiling, stirring constantly. Stir in cornstarch mixture; heat to a rolling boil over high heat, stirring constantly. (If broth is not heated to a rolling boil, egg will not form threads.)

Pour egg mixture slowly into broth, stirring constantly with fork, until egg forms threads. Remove gingerroot; sprinkle with green onion.

4 or 5 servings

BEEF AND WHITE RADISH SOUP

½-pound beef flank steak
1 teaspoon cornstarch
¼ teaspoon salt
1 teaspoon vegetable oil
12 ounces white radishes (about 10 radishes)*
4 cups beef broth
1 teaspoon salt
4 thin slices peeled gingerroot
2 tablespoons chopped green onions
　　(with tops)

Trim fat from beef steak; cut beef with grain into 2-inch strips. Cut strips across grain into ⅛-inch slices. Toss beef, cornstarch, ¼ teaspoon salt, and the vegetable oil. Cover and refrigerate 20 minutes.

Cut radishes diagonally into ¼-inch slices.

Heat broth to boiling in 3-quart saucepan. Add radishes, 1 teaspoon salt and the gingerroot. Heat to boiling; cover and boil 10 minutes. Add beef; stir to separate pieces. Heat to boiling; boil uncovered 20 seconds or until beef is done. Remove gingerroot; stir in chopped green onions.

4 to 6 servings.

*A 10-ounce daikon can be substituted for white radishes. Cut daikon lengthwise into fourths. Cut each fourth crosswise into ¼-inch slices.

SICHUAN VEGETABLE SOUP

6 ounces lean pork boneless loin
½ teaspoon salt
1 tablespoon dry white wine
2 teaspoons cornstarch
1 teaspoon finely chopped gingerroot
⅛ teaspoon white pepper
6 medium dried black mushrooms
½ can (12-ounce size) shredded Sichuan
　　preserved vegetables
4 cups Chicken Broth (page 47)
1 teaspoon salt
1 green onion (with top), chopped

Cut pork loin into 2 × ⅛-inch strips. Toss pork, ½ teaspoon salt, the wine, cornstarch, gingerroot and white pepper. Cover and refrigerate 20 minutes.

Soak mushrooms in hot water 20 minutes or until soft; drain. Rinse in warm water; drain. Squeeze out excess moisture. Remove and discard stems; cut caps into ⅛-inch strips. Rinse vegetables; drain.

Heat broth and mushrooms to boiling in 3-quart saucepan. Stir in pork, vegetables and 1 teaspoon salt. Heat to boiling; reduce heat. Cover and simmer 2 minutes. Remove from heat; stir in green onion.

4 or 5 servings

Hot preserved vegetables add a delightful crunch as well as a salty aftertaste. The Sichuan preserved vegetables are available either whole or shredded. If using whole, be sure to rinse off the excess chili paste before using. You may want to omit the 1 teaspoon of salt if you use canned chicken broth.

HOT-AND-SOUR SOUP

¼ pound pork boneless loin
½ teaspoon cornstarch
½ teaspoon salt
½ teaspoon soy sauce
6 medium dried black mushrooms
4-ounce block firm tofu
4 cups Chicken Broth (page 47)
3 tablespoons white vinegar
1 tablespoon soy sauce
1 teaspoon salt
½ cup shredded canned bamboo shoots
2 tablespoons cornstarch
2 tablespoons cold water
¼ teaspoon white pepper
2 eggs, slightly beaten
2 tablespoons chopped green onion
    (with tops)
2 teaspoons red pepper sauce
½ teaspoon sesame oil

Trim fat from pork loin; cut pork with grain into 2-inch strips. Cut strips across grain into ⅛-inch slices. Stack slices; cut into thin strips. Toss pork, ½ teaspoon cornstarch, ½ teaspoon salt and ½ teaspoon soy sauce in medium bowl. Cover and refrigerate 15 minutes.

Soak mushrooms in hot water 20 minutes or until soft; drain. Rinse in warm water; drain. Squeeze out excess moisture. Remove and discard stems; cut caps into thin slices. Cut tofu into 1½ × ¼-inch pieces.

Heat broth, vinegar, 1 tablespoon soy sauce and 1 teaspoon salt to boiling in 3-quart saucepan. Stir in bamboo shoots, mushrooms, pork and tofu. Heat to boiling; reduce heat. Cover and simmer 5 minutes.

Mix 2 tablespoons cornstarch, the water and white pepper; stir into soup. Heat to rolling boil over high heat, stirring constantly. (If broth is not heated to a rolling boil, egg will not form threads.) Pour egg slowly into soup, stirring constantly with fork until egg forms threads. Stir in green onions, pepper sauce and sesame oil.

5 servings

MEATBALLS WITH CELERY CABBAGE SOUP

6 ounces celery cabbage
6 ounces lean ground pork
1 egg white
1 tablespoon cornstarch
2 teaspoons sweet white wine
1 teaspoon light soy sauce
⅛ teaspoon white pepper
4 cups Chicken Broth (page 47) or pork broth
1 teaspoon salt

Cut celery cabbage into ¾-inch pieces. Mix pork, egg white, cornstarch, wine, soy sauce, and white pepper; shape into ten 1-inch balls.

Heat broth and salt to boiling in 3-quart saucepan. Add celery cabbage; boil uncovered 2 minutes. Add meatballs; heat to boiling. Reduce heat, cover and simmer 2 minutes or until meatballs are done.

4 or 5 servings

Meatballs with Celery Cabbage Soup

WONTON SOUP

¼ pound raw medium shrimp (in shells)

2 ounces lean ground pork

3 whole water chestnuts, finely chopped

2 green onions (with tops), chopped

1 teaspoon cornstarch

½ teaspoon salt

¼ teaspoon sesame oil

Dash of white pepper

24 wonton skins

1 egg white, slightly beaten

5 cups water

½ chicken breast (about ½ pound)

½ teaspoon cornstarch

½ teaspoon salt

Dash of white pepper

4 ounces Chinese pea pods

4 ounces mushrooms

4 cups Chicken Broth (page 47)

¼ cup sliced canned bamboo shoots

1 teaspoon salt

Dash of white pepper

2 tablespoons chopped green onions
    (with tops)

¼ teaspoon sesame oil

Peel shrimp. Make a shallow cut lengthwise down back of each shrimp; wash out vein. Chop shrimp finely. Mix shrimp, pork, water chestnuts, 2 green onions, 1 teaspoon cornstarch, ½ teaspoon salt, ¼ teaspoon sesame oil and dash of white pepper.

Place ½ teaspoon shrimp mixture in center of wonton skin. (Cover remaining skins with plastic wrap to keep them pliable.) Fold bottom corner of wonton skin over filling to opposite corner, forming a triangle. Brush right corner of triangle with egg white. Bring corners together below filling; pinch left corner to right corner to seal (see illustration page 25). Repeat with remaining wonton skins. (Cover filled wontons with plastic wrap to keep them from drying out.)

Heat water to boiling in Dutch oven; add wontons. Heat to boiling; reduce heat. Simmer uncovered 2 minutes; drain. Rinse wontons under cold water; place in bowl and cover with iced water to keep them from sticking together.

Remove bones and skin from chicken breast; cut chicken into thin slices. Toss chicken, ½ teaspoon cornstarch, ½ teaspoon salt and dash of white pepper in medium bowl. Cover and refrigerate 20 minutes. Remove strings from pea pods. Place pea pods in boiling water. Cover and cook 1 minute; drain. Immediately rinse in cold water; drain. Cut pea pods lengthwise into halves. Cut mushrooms into ¼-inch slices.

Heat broth and mushrooms to boiling in Dutch oven. Stir in chicken; heat to boiling. Drain wontons. Stir wontons, bamboo shoots, 1 teaspoon salt and dash of white pepper into broth. Heat to boiling; reduce heat. Simmer uncovered 2 minutes. Stir in pea pods, 2 tablespoons green onions and ¼ teaspoon sesame oil.

8 servings

PORK DUMPLING SOUP

½ medium head green cabbage (about
    ½ pound)
¼ teaspoon salt
½ pound lean ground pork
½ teaspoon salt
½ egg white
1 teaspoon cornstarch
Dash of white pepper
½ teaspoon sugar
1 teaspoon dry white wine
1 green onion (with top), finely chopped
24 siu mai skins* (about ¾ pound)
7 cups Chicken Broth (right)
½ teaspoon sesame oil
1 green onion (with top), finely chopped

Place cabbage in workbowl of food processor fitted with steel blade. Cover and finely chop. Sprinkle ¼ teaspoon salt over cabbage in medium bowl. Let stand at room temperature 30 minutes. Squeeze excess water from cabbage. Mix cabbage, ground pork, ½ teaspoon salt, the egg white, cornstarch, white pepper, sugar, wine and 1 chopped green onion.

Hold siu mai skin in hand. (Cover remaining skins with plastic wrap to keep them pliable.) Wet the edge of half of the circle closest to fingers. Pinch 2 or 3 pleats into the wet edge. Place 1 heaping teaspoon pork mixture in center of skin. Fold circle in half, pressing pleated edge to unpleated edge to seal dumpling (see illustration page 21). Repeat with remaining skins. (Cover filled dumplings with plastic wrap to keep them from drying out.)

Heat broth and ½ teaspoon sesame oil to boiling in Dutch oven; reduce heat. Heat 4 cups water to boiling in 3-quart saucepan; add 12 dumplings. Heat to boiling. Remove dumplings with slotted spoon; place in hot broth. Repeat with remaining dumplings.

For each serving, place 1 drop sesame oil in soup bowl. Add 4 dumplings and broth; sprinkle with chopped green onion.

6 servings

*Wonton skins can be substituted for siu mai skins. Cut off corners to make a circle.

(陳) *Siu mai skins are thinner than wontons and are round instead of square. If you can't find them, you can cut circles out of wonton skins and use them as a substitute. Pleat one side and fold over into a decorative half-moon shape.*

CHICKEN BROTH

Giblets and bones from boned chicken
2 slices peeled gingerroot

Cover giblets, bones and gingerroot with boiling water. Heat to boiling; reduce heat. Cover and simmer 1½ to 2 hours. Strain broth; serve immediately or use for cooking.

Broth can be covered and refrigerated up to 4 days or frozen up to 6 months. Dip frozen container into hot water just to loosen. Place frozen block in saucepan. Cover tightly; heat, stirring occasionally, until thawed.

3

雞鴨

CHICKEN AND DUCK

SPICY CHICKEN WITH BROCCOLI

2 whole chicken breasts (about 2 pounds)
2 teaspoons cornstarch
½ teaspoon salt
¼ teaspoon white pepper
1 pound broccoli
3 green onions (with tops)
1 hot green chili or 1 teaspoon dried red
    pepper flakes
3 tablespoons vegetable oil
2 tablespoons brown bean sauce
2 teaspoons finely chopped garlic
1 teaspoon sugar
1 teaspoon finely chopped gingerroot

Remove bones and skin from chicken breasts; cut chicken into 2 × ½-inch pieces. Toss chicken, cornstarch, salt and white pepper in medium bowl. Cover and refrigerate 20 minutes.

Pare outer layer from broccoli. Cut broccoli lengthwise into 1-inch-thick stems; remove flowerets. Cut stems diagonally into ¼-inch slices. Place broccoli flowerets and stems in boiling water; heat to boiling. Cover and cook 1 minute; drain. Immediately rinse in cold water; drain. Cut green onions diagonally into 1-inch pieces. Remove seeds and membranes from chili. Cut chili into very thin slices.

Heat wok until very hot. Add 3 tablespoons vegetable oil; tilt wok to coat side. Add chili, brown bean sauce, garlic, sugar and gingerroot; stir-fry 10 seconds. Add chicken; stir-fry 2 minutes or until chicken is white. Add broccoli and green onions; stir-fry 1 minute or until broccoli is hot.

4 servings

CHICKEN ALMOND DING

2 whole chicken breasts (about 2 pounds)
1 egg white
1 teaspoon salt
1 teaspoon cornstarch
1 teaspoon soy sauce
Dash of white pepper
2 medium carrots
2 tablespoons oyster sauce or 1 tablespoon
    dark soy sauce
1 tablespoon plus 1 teaspoon cornstarch
¼ teaspoon water
Vegetable oil
2 tablespoons vegetable oil
½ cup blanched whole almonds
¼ cup diced onion
1 teaspoon finely chopped garlic
1 teaspoon finely chopped gingerroot
1 cup diced celery
½ cup diced water chestnuts
1 teaspoon salt
½ cup diced canned bamboo shoots
1 can (4 ounces) button mushrooms, drained
½ cup Chicken Broth (page 47)
1 cup frozen peas
2 tablespoons chopped green onions
    (with tops)

Remove bones and skin from chicken breasts;
cut chicken into ½-inch pieces. Mix egg white,
1 teaspoon salt, 1 teaspoon cornstarch, the
soy sauce and white pepper in medium bowl;
stir in chicken. Cover and refrigerate 30
minutes.

Cut carrots into ½-inch pieces. Place carrots
in boiling water; heat to boiling. Cover and
cook 1 minute. Immediately rinse in cold water; drain. Mix oyster sauce, 1 tablespoon plus
1 teaspoon cornstarch and the water.

Heat vegetable oil (1 inch) in wok to 325°.
Add chicken pieces; fry until chicken turns
white, stirring to separate pieces. Remove
chicken from wok; drain. Wash and thoroughly dry wok.

Heat wok until very hot. Add 2 tablespoons
vegetable oil; tilt wok to coat side. Add almonds; stir-fry 1 minute or until golden
brown. Remove almonds from wok; drain on
paper towels. Add onion, garlic and gingerroot; stir-fry until garlic is light brown. Add
celery, water chestnuts and 1 teaspoon salt;
stir-fry 1 minute. Add bamboo shoots and
mushrooms; stir-fry 1 minute. Stir in carrots,
chicken and broth. Heat to boiling; cover and
cook 2 minutes. Stir in cornstarch mixture;
cook and stir 20 seconds or until thickened.
Stir in peas. Garnish with almonds and green
onions.

4 servings

WALNUT CHICKEN

2 cups water
1 cup walnuts
¼ teaspoon sugar
2 whole chicken breasts (about 2 pounds)
1 egg white
2 teaspoons cornstarch
1 teaspoon salt
⅛ teaspoon white pepper
2 ounces Chinese pea pods
2 stalks celery
2 green onions (with tops)
2 tablespoons oyster sauce
1 tablespoon cornstarch
1 tablespoon water
1 cup vegetable oil
½ cup Chicken Broth (page 47)
1 tablespoon diced pimiento

Heat 2 cups water to boiling; add walnuts. heat to boiling; boil 1 minute. Drain; rinse under cold water. Remove skin from walnuts; sprinkle walnuts with sugar.

Remove bones and skin from chicken breasts; cut chicken into ¾-inch pieces. Mix egg white, 2 teaspoons cornstarch, the salt and white pepper in medium bowl; stir in chicken. Cover and refrigerate 20 minutes.

Remove strings from pea pods; cut large pea pods into 3 pieces. Place pea pods in boiling water; heat to boiling. Boil 30 seconds; drain. Immediately rinse in cold water. Cut celery diagonally into ¼-inch slices. Cut green onions diagonally into 1-inch pieces. Mix oyster sauce, 1 tablespoon cornstarch and 1 tablespoon water.

Heat vegetable oil in wok to 350° Add walnuts; fry until walnuts are light brown. Remove walnuts from oil, using slotted spoon; drain on paper towels.

Heat vegetable oil to 350°. Add chicken; fry until chicken turns white, stirring to separate pieces. Remove chicken from oil, using slotted spoon; drain on paper towels. Pour oil from wok, reserving 2 tablespoons.

Heat wok until very hot. Add 2 tablespoons reserved vegetable oil; tilt wok to coat side. Add celery; stir-fry 1 minute. Add broth; heat to boiling. Cover and simmer 1 minute. Add chicken, pea pods, green onions and pimiento; heat to boiling. Stir in cornstarch mixture; cook and stir until mixture thickens. Stir in walnuts.

4 servings

Use a paring knife to loosen and remove skins from blanched walnuts. The walnuts must be hot for the skins to come off easily.

SPICY CHICKEN WITH CELERY

2 whole chicken breasts (about 2 pounds)
2 teaspoons cornstarch
½ teaspoon salt
¼ teaspoon white pepper
5 stalks celery
3 green onions (with tops)
1 hot green chili or 1 teaspoon dried red
    pepper flakes
3 tablespoons vegetable oil
2 tablespoons brown bean sauce
2 teaspoons finely chopped garlic
1 teaspoon finely chopped gingerroot

Remove bones and skin from chicken breasts; cut chicken into 2 × ½-inch strips. Toss chicken, cornstarch, salt and white pepper in medium bowl. Cover and refrigerate 20 minutes.

Cut celery diagonally into ¼-inch slices. Place celery in boiling water; heat to boiling. Boil 1 minute; drain. Immediately rinse in cold water; drain. Cut green onions diagonally into 1-inch pieces. Remove stems and membranes from chili. Cut chili into very thin slices.

Heat wok until very hot. Add vegetable oil; tilt wok to coat side. Add bean sauce, chili, garlic and gingerroot; stir-fry 10 seconds. Add chicken; stir-fry until chicken turns white. Add green onions and celery; stir-fry 1 minute.

4 servings

This recipe is especially nice because celery is readily available, in any season. Traditionally, celery was not used in Chinese cooking, but during a recent trip to China, I discovered celery being served in the best restaurants. Add celery to other Chinese recipes, if you like. Hold the stem of a hot green chili and cut off the tip with scissors. Loosen the membranes and seeds with tip of scissor blade; discard. Cut chili into thin slices with scissors.

SICHUAN CHICKEN WITH CASHEWS

2 whole chicken breasts (about 2 pounds)
1 egg white
1 teaspoon cornstarch
1 teaspoon soy sauce
Dash of white pepper
1 large green bell pepper
1 medium onion
1 can (8½ ounces) sliced bamboo shoots,
    drained
1 tablespoon cornstarch
1 tablespoon cold water
1 tablespoon soy sauce
2 tablespoons vegetable oil
1 cup raw cashews
¼ teaspoon salt
2 tablespoons vegetable oil
1 teaspoon finely chopped gingerroot
1 tablespoon Hoisin sauce
2 teaspoons chili paste
¼ cup chicken broth
2 tablespoons chopped green onion (with
    tops)

Remove bones and skin from chicken breasts; cut chicken into ¾-inch pieces. Mix egg white, 1 teaspoon cornstarch, 1 teaspoon soy sauce and the white pepper in medium bowl; stir in chicken. Cover and refrigerate 20 minutes.

Cut bell pepper into ¾-inch pieces. Cut onion into 8 pieces. Cut bamboo shoots into ½-inch pieces. Mix 1 tablespoon cornstarch, the water and 1 tablespoon soy sauce.

Heat wok until very hot. Add 2 tablespoons vegetable oil; tilt wok to coat side. Add cashews; stir-fry 1 minute or until cashews are light brown. Remove cashews from wok; drain on paper towel. Sprinkle with salt. Add chicken to wok; stir-fry until chicken turns white. Remove chicken from wok.

Add 2 tablespoons vegetable oil; tilt wok to coat side. Add onion pieces and gingerroot; stir-fry until gingerroot is light brown. Add chicken, bell pepper, bamboo shoots, Hoisin sauce and chili paste; stir-fry 1 minute. Add broth; heat to boiling. Stir in cornstarch mixture; cook and stir 20 seconds or until thickened. Stir in cashews and green onions.

4 servings

In this recipe, the method of coating chicken pieces in a cornstarch batter and then stir-frying them twice produces well-sealed, tender morsels. You'll find raw cashews are readily available in health food stores or Oriental markets.

SHREDDED CHICKEN WITH BEAN SPROUTS AND PEA PODS

2 whole chicken breasts (about 2 pounds)
1 teaspoon cornstarch
½ teaspoon salt
⅛ teaspoon white pepper
4 ounces Chinese pea pods
1 pound bean sprouts
2 tablespoons chicken broth
1 tablespoon dark soy sauce
2 teaspoons cornstarch
1 teaspoon sugar
1 tablespoon vegetable oil
½ teaspoon salt
2 tablespoons vegetable oil
2 teaspoons finely chopped garlic
1 teaspoon finely chopped gingerroot
¼ cup chicken broth

Remove bones and skin from chicken breasts; cut chicken into 2 × ½-inch pieces. Stack slices; cut into thin strips. Toss chicken, 1 teaspoon cornstarch, ½ teaspoon salt and the white pepper in medium bowl. Cover and refrigerate 30 minutes.

Remove strings from pea pods. Place pea pods in boiling water; heat to boiling. Immediately remove from heat; drain. Immediately rinse in cold water; drain. Rinse bean sprouts in cold water; drain throughly. Mix 2 tablespoons broth, the soy sauce, 2 teaspoons cornstarch and the sugar.

Heat wok until very hot. Add 1 tablespoon vegetable oil; tilt wok to coat side. Add bean sprouts and ½ teaspoon salt; stir-fry 2 minutes. Remove bean sprouts from wok; drain.

Heat wok until very hot. Add 2 tablespoons vegetable oil; tilt wok to coat side. Add chicken, garlic and gingerroot; stir-fry 2 minutes or until chicken turns white. Add bean sprouts and pea pods; stir-fry 1 minute. Add ¼ cup broth; heat to boiling. Stir in cornstarch mixture; cook and stir until thickened.

4 servings

 Bean sprouts and pea pods are typical Chinese vegetables that add both flavor and texture to many recipes. Take care not to overcook the sprouts or they will become soggy and limp. Briefly stir-fried, they'll stay plump and crisp.

CUBED CHICKEN IN BROWN BEAN SAUCE

2 whole chicken breasts (about 2 pounds)
2 teaspoons cornstarch
½ teaspoon salt
6 green onions (with tops)
3 tablespoons vegetable oil
2 tablespoons vegetable oil
2 tablespoons brown bean sauce
2 teaspoons sugar
2 teaspoons finely chopped garlic
1 teaspoon finely chopped gingerroot

Remove bones and skin from chicken breasts; cut chicken into 1-inch pieces. Toss chicken, cornstarch and salt. Cover and refrigerate 20 minutes. Cut green onions diagonally into 1-inch pieces.

Heat wok until very hot. Add 3 tablespoons vegetable oil; tilt wok to coat side. Add chicken; stir-fry until chicken turns white, separating chicken pieces. Remove chicken from wok.

Heat wok until very hot. Add 2 tablespoons vegetable oil; tilt wok to coat side. Add bean sauce, sugar, garlic and gingerroot; stir-fry 30 seconds or until well mixed. Add chicken; stir-fry 2 minutes. Add green onions; stir-fry 30 seconds.

4 servings

LEMON CHICKEN

2 whole chicken breasts (about 2 pounds)
1 egg
2 teaspoons cornstarch
1 teaspoon salt
¼ teaspoon white pepper
1 teaspoon finely chopped gingerroot
1 tablespoon cornstarch
1 tablespoon water
Vegetable oil
¼ cup all-purpose flour
¼ cup water
2 tablespoons cornstarch
2 tablespoons vegetable oil
¼ teaspoon baking soda
¼ teaspoon salt
⅓ cup chicken broth
¼ cup sugar
3 tablespoons lemon juice
2 tablespoons light corn syrup
2 tablespoons vinegar
1 tablespoon vegetable oil
1 teaspoon dark soy sauce
1 teaspoon finely chopped garlic
½ lemon, thinly sliced

Remove bones and skin from chicken breasts; cut each chicken breast lengthwise into fourths. Place chicken in a shallow dish. Mix egg, 2 teaspoons cornstarch, 1 teaspoon salt, the white pepper and gingerroot. Pour egg mixture over chicken, turning chicken to coat all sides. Cover and refrigerate 30 minutes. Remove chicken from marinade; reserve marinade. Mix 1 tablespoon cornstarch and 1 tablespoon water.

Heat vegetable oil (1½ inches) in wok to 350°. Mix reserved marinade, the flour, ¼ cup water, 2 tablespoons cornstarch, 2 tablespoons vegetable oil, the baking soda and ¼ teaspoon salt. Dip chicken pieces, one at a time, into batter to coat all sides. Fry 2 pieces at a time 3 minutes or until light brown; drain on paper towels.

Increase oil temperature to 375°. Fry all the chicken 2 minutes or until golden brown, turning once, drain on paper towels. Cut each piece crosswise into ½-inch pieces, using a very sharp knife; place in a single layer on heated platter.

Heat broth, sugar, lemon juice, corn syrup, vinegar, 1 tablespoon vegetable oil, the soy sauce and garlic to boiling. Stir in cornstarch mixture; cook and stir 10 seconds or until thickened. Simmer uncovered 30 seconds. Pour sauce over chicken; garnish with lemon slices and, if desired, maraschino cherries or cilantro.

6 servings

(陳) *There are a number of different Lemon Chicken recipes in the Chinese repertoire. This popular version develops an intense lemony flavor without lengthy marinating. After frying, you can refrigerate the chicken for 24 hours if you choose. Make the sauce ahead, too, if it's more convenient. Just before serving, heat oil to 375° and fry chicken, turning once or twice, for about 2 minutes. Reheat sauce to boiling and serve over chicken.*

SESAME CHICKEN WITH FUN SEE

2 whole chicken breasts (about 2 pounds)
1 egg
2 tablespoons all-purpose flour
2 tablespoons cornstarch
2 tablespoons water
1 teaspoon salt
2 teaspoons vegetable oil
¼ teaspoon baking soda
¼ teaspoon white pepper
½ cup water
¼ cup cornstarch
1 cup sugar
1 cup Chicken Broth (page 47)
¾ cup vinegar
2 teaspoons dark soy sauce
2 teaspoons chili paste
1 teaspoon vegetable oil
1 clove garlic, finely chopped
Vegetable oil
2 ounces cellophane or rice stick noodles
2 tablespoons Toasted Sesame Seed (page 34)

Remove bones and skin from chicken breasts; cut chicken into 2 × ½-inch strips. Mix egg, flour, 2 tablespoons cornstarch, 2 tablespoons water, the salt, 2 teaspoons vegetable oil, the baking soda and white pepper; stir in chicken. Cover and refrigerate 20 minutes. Mix ½ cup water and ¼ cup cornstarch.

Heat sugar, broth, vinegar, soy sauce, chili paste, 1 teaspoon vegetable oil and the garlic to boiling. Stir in cornstarch mixture; cook and stir until thickened. Remove from heat; keep warm.

Heat vegetable oil (1½ inches) in wok to 350°. Pull noodles apart gently. Fry ¼ of the noodles at a time 5 seconds or until puffed, turning once; drain on paper towels.

Heat oil to 350°. Fry about 10 pieces of chicken, adding 1 at a time, 3 minutes or until light brown. Remove from oil, using slotted spoon; drain on paper towels. Repeat with remaining chicken.

Heat oil to 375°. Fry about ⅓ of the chicken 1 minute or until golden brown. Remove from oil, using slotted spoon; drain on paper towels. Repeat with remaining chicken. Place chicken on heated platter.

Heat sauce to boiling; pour over chicken. Sprinkle with sesame seed. Arrange cellophane noodles around chicken.

6 servings

A Chinese saying claims that sesame seed improves the spirits; it assuredly improves flavors and is very important in Cantonese cooking but is also featured in the cuisines of other regions. The quickly fried cellophane noodles here (fun see) add crunch to this hot-and-sour dish.

BIRD OF PARADISE CHICKEN

1 green onion (with top)

4 whole chicken breasts (about 4 pounds)

8 thin slices Virginia ham (about 4 ounces)

2 tablespoons cornstarch

2 tablespoons water

½ teaspoon sugar

1½ cups Chicken Broth (page 47)

¼ cup sliced canned bamboo shoots

2 teaspoons dark soy sauce

Dash of white pepper

1 teaspoon sesame oil

Vegetable oil

¼ cup all-purpose flour

¼ cup water

2 tablespoons cornstarch

2 tablespoons vegetable oil

1 teaspoon gingerroot juice (page 9)

¼ teaspoon baking soda

¼ teaspoon salt

1 egg white

Cut green onion into 1-inch pieces; shred pieces lengthwise into fine strips. Cover with iced water; let stand 10 minutes or until strips curl.

Remove bones and skin from chicken breasts; cut each chicken breast lengthwise into halves. To butterfly chicken, split each piece lengthwise almost into halves; open flat. Place 1 ham slice on each chicken piece; fold chicken lengthwise in half, pressing cut edge to seal. Mix 2 tablespoons cornstarch, 2 tablespoons water and the sugar.

Heat broth, bamboo shoots, dark soy sauce, white pepper and sesame oil to boiling. Stir in cornstarch mixture; cook and stir 1 minute or until thickened. Remove from heat; keep warm.

Heat vegetable oil (2 inches) in wok to 350°. Mix flour, ¼ cup water, 2 tablespoons cornstarch, 2 tablespoons vegetable oil, the gingerroot juice, baking soda, salt and egg white in medium bowl. Dip chicken, 1 piece at a time, into batter to coat all sides. Fry 2 pieces at a time 3 minutes or until very light brown; drain on paper towels.

Increase oil temperature to 375°. Fry half the chicken 2 minutes or until golden brown, turning once; drain on paper towels. Repeat with remaining chicken. Cut each piece crosswise into 1-inch pieces, using a very sharp knife; place in a single layer on heated platter. Pour sauce over chicken; garnish with green onion.

8 servings

陳 *Crisply batter fried on the outside with a fine slice of firm Virginia ham down the middle, this colorful dish makes a most impressive presentation. Garnish with curly scallion ringlets. If necessary, secure edges of chicken together with wooden picks.*

Bird of Paradise Chicken and Chicken with Pickled Ginger Sauce (page 61)

COCONUT CHICKEN

2 tablespoons shredded coconut
4 whole chicken breasts (about 4 pounds)
1 cup canned coconut milk
½ cup Chicken Broth (page 47)
¼ cup sugar
2 tablespoons lemon juice
1 tablespoon plus 1½ teaspoons
    cornstarch
2 teaspoons gingerroot juice (page 9)
2 teaspoons vegetable oil
1 teaspoon salt
⅛ teaspoon white pepper
Vegetable oil
¼ cup all-purpose flour
¼ cup water
2 tablespoons cornstarch
2 tablespoons vegetable oil
¼ teaspoon baking soda
¼ teaspoon salt
1 egg white

Heat oven to 300°. Bake coconut, stirring occasionally, 10 minutes or until golden brown. (Watch carefully so coconut does not burn.) Remove bones and skin from chicken breast; cut each chicken breast lengthwise into 2-inch strips.

Heat coconut milk, broth, sugar, lemon juice, 1 tablespoon plus 1½ teaspoons cornstarch, the gingerroot juice, 2 teaspoons vegetable oil, 1 teaspoon salt and the white pepper to boiling. Cook, stirring constantly, until thickened. Remove from heat; keep warm.

Heat vegetable oil (2 inches) in wok to 350°. Mix flour, water, 2 tablespoons cornstarch, 2 tablespoons vegetable oil, the baking soda, ¼ teaspoon salt and the egg white in medium bowl. Dip chicken, 1 piece at a time, into batter to coat all sides. Fry 2 pieces at a time 3 minutes or until very light brown; drain on paper towels.

Increase oil to 375°. Fry half of the chicken 2 minutes or until golden brown, turning once; drain on paper towels. Repeat with remaining chicken. Cut each piece crosswise into 1-inch pieces, using a very sharp knife; place in a single layer on heated platter. Pour coconut sauce over chicken; garnish with toasted coconut and, if desired, maraschino cherries.

8 servings

The coconut flavor of this recipe turns everyday chicken into an exotic tropical treat. The white sauce over golden brown chicken makes a very attractive dish. Toasted coconut stores well at room temperature. Keep it in a closed jar up to several months.

CHICKEN WITH PICKLED GINGER SAUCE

6 chicken thighs (about 1 pound)
½ teaspoon salt
½ teaspoon light soy sauce
¼ teaspoon white pepper
½ cup pickled young gingerroot
2 green onions (with tops)
1 small dill pickle
2 tablespoons cornstarch
2 tablespoons water
2 tablespoons vinegar
2 teaspoons sugar
2 teaspoons finely chopped garlic
1 teaspoon finely chopped gingerroot
2 teaspoons dry white wine
2 teaspoons soy sauce
1 teaspoon sesame oil
3 cups vegetable oil
1 tablespoon cornstarch
2 tablespoons vegetable oil
1¼ cups Chicken Broth (page 47)

Cut each chicken thigh lengthwise down center to bone; loosen bone and remove. Mix salt, ½ teaspoon soy sauce and the white pepper; rub mixture on chicken skin. Place chicken on rack; refrigerate uncovered 1 hour.

Cut pickled gingerroot into thin strips. Cut green onions into 2-inch pieces; shred lengthwise into fine strips. Cover with iced water; let stand 10 minutes or until strips curl. Cut pickle lengthwise into thin strips. Mix 2 tablespoons cornstarch and the water.

Mix vinegar, sugar, garlic, gingerroot, wine, 2 teaspoons soy sauce and the sesame oil.

Heat 3 cups vegetable oil in wok to 350°. Sprinkle 1 tablespoon cornstarch evenly over chicken. Fry chicken 4 minutes or until golden brown. Remove chicken, using slotted spoon; drain on paper towels. Cut each chicken thigh lengthwise into 3 or 4 pieces. Keep chicken warm on heatproof platter in 250° oven. Pour oil from wok.

Heat wok until very hot. Add 2 tablespoons vegetable oil; tilt wok to coat side. Carefully stir in vinegar mixture; cook 1 minute. Add broth; heat to boiling. Stir in cornstarch mixture; cook and stir until thickened. Stir in pickled gingerroot and pickle. Pour sauce over chicken; garnish with green onions.

4 servings

 Pickled ginger is made from young ginger. It is very tender and so mild, you could eat it plain, not just use it as a seasoning. Young ginger can be purchased in the spring but may be hard to find. You can pickle your own young ginger or purchase it at a Chinese grocery.

STIR-FRIED CHICKEN WITH CUCUMBERS

6 chicken thighs (about 1 pound)
1 tablespoon cornstarch
½ teaspoon salt
⅛ teaspoon white pepper
6 medium dried black mushrooms
1 medium cucumber
6 green onions (with tops)
1 tablespoon dry white wine
1 tablespoon soy sauce
1 teaspoon sugar
1 teaspoon cornstarch
3 tablespoons vegetable oil
1 teaspoon finely chopped gingerroot
1 teaspoon finely chopped garlic

Remove bones and skin from chicken thighs; cut chicken into 1 × ½-inch pieces. Toss chicken, 1 tablespoon cornstarch, the salt and white pepper in medium bowl. Cover and refrigerate 20 minutes.

Soak mushrooms in hot water 20 minutes or until soft; drain. Rinse in warm water; drain. Squeeze out excess moisture. Remove and discard stems; cut caps into ¼-inch slices. Pare cucumber; cut lengthwise into halves. Remove seeds; cut cucumber diagonally into ¼-inch-thick slices. Cut green onions diagonally into 1-inch pieces. Mix wine, soy sauce, sugar and 1 teaspoon cornstarch.

Heat wok until very hot. Add vegetable oil; tilt wok to coat side. Add chicken, mushrooms, gingerroot and garlic; stir-fry 2 minutes, separating chicken pieces. Add cucumber; stir-fry 1 minute. Add green onions and soy sauce mixture; cook and stir 1 minute.

4 servings

 Chicken breasts can be used instead of the thighs. You will need 2 whole chicken breasts (about 2 pounds). To remove bones from chicken thighs, cut down the center of the thigh to the bone; separate the meat from the bone. Cucumbers are generally eaten raw in United States, but they are luscious cooked with chicken.

SPICY CHICKEN WITH CABBAGE

6 chicken thighs (about 1 pound)
2 tablespoons cornstarch
1 teaspoon salt
⅛ teaspoon white pepper
8 dried black mushrooms
½ medium head cabbage
4 green onions (with tops)
1 medium red bell pepper
2 teaspoons cornstarch
1 teaspoon sugar
2 teaspoons water
2 teaspoons finely chopped garlic
2 teaspoons finely chopped gingerroot
2 teaspoons chili paste
2 teaspoons soy sauce
3 tablespoons vegetable oil
3 tablespoons vegetable oil
¼ cup chicken broth

Remove bones and skin from chicken thighs; cut chicken into 1 × ½-inch pieces. Toss chicken, 2 tablespoons cornstarch, the salt and white pepper in medium bowl. Cover and refrigerate 20 minutes.

Soak mushrooms in hot water 20 minutes or until soft; drain. Rinse in warm water; drain. Squeeze out excess moisture. Remove and discard stems; cut caps into ½-inch pieces.

Cut cabbage into 1-inch pieces. Cut green onions diagonally into 1-inch pieces. Cut bell pepper into 1-inch pieces. Mix 2 teaspoons cornstarch, the sugar and water. Mix garlic, gingerroot, chili paste and soy sauce.

Heat wok until very hot. Add 3 tablespoons oil; tilt wok to coat side. Add chicken; stir-fry 2 minutes or until chicken turns white. Remove chicken from wok. (If particles of chicken stick to wok, wash and thoroughly dry wok.)

Heat wok until very hot. Add 3 tablespoons vegetable oil; tilt wok to coat side. Add mushrooms, cabbage and the garlic mixture; stir-fry 2 minutes. Add broth; cook and stir 2 minutes. Stir in cornstarch mixture; cook and stir 10 seconds or until thickened. Add chicken, green onions and bell pepper; cook and stir 2 minutes or until chicken mixture is evenly coated. Increase heat to high; stir-fry until excess moisture evaporates.

4 servings

CHICKEN WITH OYSTERS

6 chicken thighs (about 1 pound)
1 tablespoon cornstarch
½ teaspoon salt
⅛ teaspoon white pepper
6 dried black mushrooms
1 pint shucked oysters, drained
¼ cup cornstarch
1 teaspoon sesame oil
2 tablespoons cornstarch
½ teaspoon white pepper
6 green onions (with tops)
3 tablespoons vegetable oil
2 tablespoons vegetable oil
2 teaspoons finely chopped gingerroot
2 teaspoons finely chopped garlic
2 tablespoons sweet white wine
2 tablespoons mushroom soy sauce

Remove bones and skin from chicken thighs; cut chicken into 1 × ½-inch pieces. Toss chicken, 1 tablespoon cornstarch, the salt and ⅛ teaspoon white pepper in medium bowl. Cover and refrigerate 20 minutes.

Soak mushrooms in hot water 20 minutes or until soft; drain. Rinse in warm water; drain. Squeeze out excess moisture. Remove and discard stems; cut caps into ½-inch pieces. Rinse oysters in cold water; drain. Toss oysters and ¼ cup cornstarch; rinse in cold water to remove cornstarch. Pat dry with paper towels. Gently toss oysters with sesame oil. Toss oysters, 2 tablespoons cornstarch and ½ teaspoon white pepper until oysters are evenly coated. Cut green onions diagonally into 1-inch pieces.

Heat wok until very hot. Add 3 tablespoons vegetable oil; tilt wok to coat side. Add chicken and mushrooms; stir-fry 2 minutes, separating chicken pieces. Remove chicken mixture from wok. Wash and thoroughly dry wok.

Heat wok until very hot. Add 2 tablespoons vegetable oil; tilt wok to coat side. Add green onions, gingerroot and garlic; stir-fry 10 seconds. Add oysters; gently stir-fry 1 minute. Add chicken mixture; stir-fry 1 minute. Stir in wine and soy sauce.

4 servings

Be sure to separate the chicken pieces when adding to the hot oil. If you don't, they will stick together because of the cornstarch. Be sure the wok is very hot, or the oysters will cook too slowly. Stir-fry oysters very gently so they don't break.

CORNISH HENS WITH SOY SAUCE

4 frozen Rock Cornish hens, thawed
2 cups soy sauce
2 cups water
½ cup dry white wine
1 cup sugar
½ cup honey
8 to 10 one-by-one-eighth-inch pieces
    gingerroot
Green Onion Flowers (right)

Remove excess fat from Cornish hens. Wash hens in cold running water; drain.

Heat soy sauce, water, wine, sugar, honey and gingerroot to boiling in 3-quart saucepan. Add 1 hen; turn hen over, being careful not to break skin. Reduce heat to medium; simmer 5 minutes. Reduce heat to low; cover and simmer 5 minutes or until done. Remove hen carefully to prevent breaking skin; keep warm. Repeat with remaining hens. (If soy sauce mixture does not cover hen, turn hen 2 or 3 times and simmer 10 minutes. Do not allow the mixture to boil too hard, or the skin on the hens will break.) Cut each hen into halves. Garnish with Green Onion Flowers.

4 servings

SOY SAUCE CHICKEN

4 cups mushroom soy sauce
3 cups water
1 cup dry white wine
½ cup sugar
5 thin slices fresh gingerroot
4 star anise
3-pound whole broiler-fryer chicken
Green Onion Flowers (below)
    or parsley

Heat soy sauce, water, wine, sugar, gingerroot and star anise to boiling in Dutch oven. Add chicken; heat to boiling. Reduce heat to medium-low; cover and simmer 30 minutes or until done, turning chicken and stirring mixture 2 or 3 times.

Remove chicken from soy sauce mixture; let chicken stand 20 minutes. Chop chicken with cleaver into 2 × 1-inch pieces. Arrange pieces on serving platter in the shape of a chicken; garnish with Green Onion Flowers.

4 servings

Green Onion Flowers

4 green onions

For each flower, remove root and green top from 1 green onion. Cut onion into 3-inch piece. Make 4 cross cuts about ¾-inch deep on one end; repeat on other end. Place onion in iced water about 10 minutes or until ends curl.

Leftover soy sauce mixture may be saved in the refrigerator and used to make this recipe again. A pork roast can be prepared using this soy sauce mixture. In that case, increase the simmering time to 1 hour.

STIR-FRIED CHICKEN LIVERS AND VEGETABLES

10 ounces chicken livers
2 teaspoons cornstarch
1 teaspoon sesame oil
⅛ teaspoon white pepper
8 ounces celery cabbage
¼ cup chicken broth
1 tablespoon cornstarch
1 teaspoon sugar
1 teaspoon light soy sauce
3 tablespoons vegetable oil
1 tablespoon vegetable oil
1 teaspoon salt
2 tablespoons vegetable oil
2 teaspoons finely chopped garlic
1 teaspoon finely chopped gingerroot

Cut each chicken liver into fourths. Toss chicken livers, 2 teaspoons cornstarch, the sesame oil and white pepper in medium bowl. Cut celery cabbage crosswise into 1-inch strips. Mix broth, 1 tablespoon cornstarch, the sugar and soy sauce.

Heat wok until very hot. Add 3 tablespoons vegetable oil; tilt wok to coat side. Add chicken livers; stir-fry 2 minutes or until firm and no longer pink. Remove chicken livers from wok; drain.

Heat wok until very hot. Add 1 tablespoon vegetable oil; tilt wok to coat side. Add celery cabbage and salt; stir-fry 2 minutes. Remove celery cabbage from wok; drain. Wash and thoroughly dry wok.

Heat wok until very hot. Add 2 tablespoons vegetable oil; tilt wok to coat side. Add chicken livers, garlic and gingerroot. Stir in cornstarch mixture; cook and stir 1 minute. Stir in celery cabbage.

4 servings

PRESSED DUCK

4½- to 5-pound duckling
1-pound pork boneless loin or leg
½ cup sliced canned bamboo shoots
2 green onions (with tops)
2 quarts water
½ cup soy sauce
4 thin slices gingerroot
3 cloves garlic, crushed
2 teaspoons salt
1 teaspoon five-spice powder
⅓ cup sifted water chestnut flour
⅓ cup cornstarch
½ teaspoon salt
2 egg whites, slightly beaten
Vegetable oil
½ cup blanched almonds
1 cup Chicken Broth (page 47)
¼ cup oyster sauce
3 tablespoons cornstarch
3 tablespoons cold water

Cut ducklings lengthwise into halves. Trim fat from pork. Cut bamboo shoots lengthwise into thin strips. Cut green onions into 2-inch pieces; cut pieces lengthwise into thin strips.

Heat 2 quarts water, the soy sauce, gingerroot, garlic, 2 teaspoons salt and the five-spice powder to boiling in Dutch oven; add duckling and pork. Heat to boiling; reduce heat. Cover and simmer 1½ hours. Remove duckling and pork; cool. Skim fat from broth. Reserve and refrigerate 1 cup broth. Remove bones from duckling, keeping meat and skin as intact as possible. Shred pork and any small pieces of remaining duckling meat from boning.

Mix water chestnut flour, ⅓ cup cornstarch and ½ teaspoon salt. Stir half of the flour mixture into shredded meat. Brush both sides of duckling halves with half of the egg whites. Sprinkle both sides of duckling with half of the remaining flour mixture. Place duckling halves, skin sides down, in greased square pan, 9 × 9 × 2 inches. Press shredded meat firmly and evenly on duckling halves. Brush with remaining egg whites; sprinkle with remaining flour mixture. Place pan on rack in steamer; cover and steam over boiling water 20 minutes. (Add boiling water if necessary.) Remove duckling from steamer; cover and refrigerate 1 hour or until cold.

Heat vegetable oil (1½ inches) in wok to 350°. Fry almonds 1 minute or until light brown. Remove almonds from wok; drain on paper towels. Chop almonds finely. Fry 1 duckling half at a time 5 minutes or until golden brown, turning once; drain on paper towels. Cut each lengthwise into halves; cut halves into ½-inch slices. Arrange on heated platter.

Heat reserved broth, the chicken broth, bamboo shoots and oyster sauce to boiling. Mix 3 tablespoons cornstarch and 3 tablespoons water; stir into broth mixture. Cook and stir until thickened; pour over duckling. Sprinkle with almonds; garnish with green onions.

8 servings

 Pressed Duck can be prepared in advance. After steaming, cover duck and reserved stock separately and refrigerate no longer than 24 hours. Just before serving, continue as directed above.

Pressed Duck and Stir-fried Green Beans with Sichuan Sauce (page 129)

4

海鮮

FISH AND SHELLFISH

HALIBUT WITH SALTED BLACK BEANS AND CHILIES

1-pound halibut steak
1 teaspoon salt
1 teaspoon finely chopped gingerroot
¼ teaspoon white pepper
1 teaspoon cornstarch
2 tablespoons salted black beans
4 green onions (with tops)
2 hot green chilies
1 tablespoon cornstarch
1 tablespoon water
1 teaspoon sugar
2 tablespoons vegetable oil
1 tablespoon vegetable oil
2 teaspoons finely chopped garlic
1 cup Chicken Broth (page 47)
Spinach or lettuce leaves

Pat fish dry with paper towels. Mix salt, gingerroot, and white pepper. Coat both sides of fish with gingerroot mixture. Rub 1 teaspoon cornstarch on both sides of fish. Cover and refrigerate 30 minutes.

Place beans in bowl; cover with warm water. Stir beans about 2 minutes to remove excess salt. Remove beans from water; drain well.

Cut 3 green onions diagonally into 1-inch pieces. Cut remaining green onion into thin slices. Remove seeds and membranes from chilies. Cut chilies into very thin slices. Mix 1 tablespoon cornstarch, the water and sugar.

Heat wok over medium heat until hot. Add 2 tablespoons vegetable oil; tilt wok to coat side. Fry fish 2 minutes or until brown, turning once. Reduce heat to low; cover and simmer 10 minutes, turning after 3 minutes. Remove fish from wok.

Heat wok until very hot. Add 1 tablespoon vegetable oil; tilt wok to coat side. Add beans, chilies, garlic and green onion pieces; stir-fry 1 minute. Add broth; heat to boiling. Stir in cornstarch mixture; cook and stir until thickened. Add fish; turn fish to coat with sauce. Heat 2 minutes. Line serving platter with spinach leaves. Place fish on spinach; sprinkle with green onion slices.

4 servings

陳 *Chinese recipes for fin fish—no matter what kind—always include gingerroot. This halibut is coated with it and then is given even more flavor with the addition of garlic, hot green chilies and black beans.*

Halibut with Salted Black Beans and Chilies

SEA BASS WITH GREEN BEANS

½ pound sea bass or walleye fillets

1 teaspoon cornstarch

1 teaspoon roasted sesame oil

½ teaspoon salt

½ teaspoon finely chopped gingerroot

Dash of white pepper

10 ounces green beans

1 green onion (with top)

1 tablespoon cornstarch

1 tablespoon water

1 teaspoon sugar

¼ teaspoon roasted sesame oil

2 tablespoons vegetable oil

2 tablespoons vegetable oil

1 teaspoon finely chopped garlic

½ teaspoon salt

½ cup Chicken Broth (page 47)

Pat fish dry with paper towels. Cut fish into 2 × ½-inch slices. Toss fish, 1 teaspoon cornstarch, 1 teaspoon sesame oil, ½ teaspoon salt, the gingerroot and white pepper in medium bowl. Cover and refrigerate 20 minutes. Snap green beans into halves. Cut green onion diagonally into 1-inch pieces. Mix 1 tablespoon cornstarch and the water. Mix sugar and ¼ teaspoon sesame oil.

Heat wok until very hot. Add 2 tablespoons vegetable oil; tilt wok to coat side. Add fish; stir-fry gently 2 minutes or until fish turns white. Remove fish from wok.

Heat wok until very hot. Add 2 tablespoons vegetable oil; tilt wok to coat side. Add green beans, garlic and ½ teaspoon salt; stir-fry 1 minute. Add broth; heat to boiling. Cover and cook 2 minutes. Stir in cornstarch mixture; cook and stir until mixture thickens. Add fish and green onion; cook and stir gently 30 seconds. Gently stir in sesame oil mixture.

4 servings

STEAMED SEA BASS

1½ pound drawn sea bass, walleye or red snapper

1 teaspoon finely chopped gingerroot

2 tablespoons vegetable oil

2 tablespoons brown bean sauce

2 cloves garlic, finely chopped

1 teaspoon salt

1 teaspoon soy sauce

¼ teaspoon roasted sesame oil

2 green onions (with tops)

Slash fish crosswise 3 times on each side. Mix gingerroot, vegetable oil, bean sauce, garlic, salt, soy sauce and sesame oil; rub cavity and outside of fish with mixture. Cover and refrigerate 40 minutes.

Cut green onions into 2-inch pieces; shred pieces lengthwise into fine strips. Cover with iced water; let stand 10 minutes or until strips curl.

Place fish on heatproof plate. Place plate on rack in steamer; cover and steam over boiling water until fish flakes easily with fork, about 15 minutes. (Add boiling water if necessary.) Garnish with green onions.

2 servings

 This recipe is an excellent one for the microwave. Place fish on microwavable platter. Cover tightly with plastic wrap, folding one corner back to allow steam to escape. Microwave on high (100%) 2 minutes. Rotate platter ½ turn. Microwave 2 minutes or until fish flakes easily with a fork. Garnish with green onions and it is ready to serve.

STIR-FRIED WALLEYE WITH CELERY CABBAGE

½ pound walleye or sea bass fillets
1 teaspoon cornstarch
1 teaspoon vegetable oil
½ teaspoon salt
½ teaspoon finely chopped gingerroot
Dash of white pepper
10 ounces celery cabbage
2 green onions (with tops)
1 tablespoon cornstarch
1 tablespoon water
3 tablespoons vegetable oil
1 teaspoon salt
1 teaspoon finely chopped garlic
¼ cup chicken broth
1 teaspoon soy sauce
¼ teaspoon roasted sesame oil

Pat fish dry with paper towels. Cut fish crosswise into 1-inch pieces. Toss fish, 1 teaspoon cornstarch, 1 teaspoon vegetable oil, ½ teaspoon salt, the gingerroot and white pepper in medium bowl. Cover and refrigerate 30 minutes.

Cut celery cabbage into ½-inch slices. Cut green onions diagonally into 2-inch pieces. Mix 1 tablespoon cornstarch and the water.

Heat wok until very hot. Add 3 tablespoons vegetable oil; tilt wok to coat side. Add fish; stir-fry gently 2 minutes or until fish turns white. Remove fish from wok.

Add 1 teaspoon salt, the garlic and celery cabbage; stir-fry 1 minute. Add broth; heat to boiling. Add cornstarch mixture; cook and stir until thickened. Stir in fish, green onions, soy sauce, and sesame oil; cook and stir 1 minute or until fish is hot.

4 servings

GLAZED WALLEYE

1 pound walleye or sea bass fillets
2 teaspoons cornstarch
½ teaspoon salt
⅛ teaspoon white pepper
2 green onions (with tops)
1 tablespoon dry white wine
1 tablespoon vinegar
1 tablespoon dark soy sauce
2 teaspoons sugar
1 teaspoon roasted sesame oil
2 tablespoons vegetable oil
1 tablespoon vegetable oil
2 teaspoons finely chopped garlic
1 teaspoon finely chopped gingerroot

Pat fish dry with paper towels. Mix cornstarch, salt and white pepper; sprinkle evenly over both sides of fish. Cover and refrigerate 20 minutes.

Cut green onions into 2-inch pieces; shred lengthwise into fine strips. Cover with iced water; let stand 10 minutes or until strips curl. Mix wine, vinegar, soy sauce, sugar and sesame oil.

Heat wok until very hot. Add 2 tablespoons vegetable oil; tilt wok to coat side. Fry fish 4 minutes or until brown, turning once. Remove fish from wok. Wash and thoroughly dry wok.

Heat wok until very hot. Add 1 tablespoon vegetable oil; tilt wok to coat side. Add garlic and gingerroot; stir-fry 30 seconds. Stir in soy sauce mixture.

Carefully add fish to wok; cook over medium heat about 2 minutes, gently spooning soy sauce mixture over fish to glaze. Garnish with green onions.

4 servings

PAN-FRIED RED SNAPPER WITH SALTED BLACK BEANS AND CHILIES

1½ pounds red snapper, walleye or sea bass
   fillets
1 teaspoon salt
1 teaspoon finely chopped gingerroot
¼ teaspoon white pepper
1 teaspoon cornstarch
2 tablespoons salted black beans
4 green onions (with tops)
2 hot green chilies
1 tablespoon cornstarch
1 tablespoon water
1 teaspoon sugar
3 tablespoons vegetable oil
2 tablespoons vegetable oil
2 teaspoons finely chopped garlic
1 cup Chicken Broth (page 47)
1 teaspoon dry white wine
1 teaspoon roasted sesame oil

Pat fish dry with paper towels. Mix salt, gingerroot, white pepper and 1 teaspoon cornstarch. Coat both sides of fish with gingerroot mixture. Cover and refrigerate 30 minutes.

Place beans in bowl; cover with warm water. Stir beans about 2 minutes to remove excess salt. Remove beans from water; drain well.

Cut 3 green onions diagonally into 1-inch pieces. Cut remaining green onion into thin slices. Remove seeds and membranes from chilies. Cut chilies into very thin slices. Mix 1 tablespoon cornstarch, the water and sugar.

Heat wok until very hot; reduce heat to medium. Add 3 tablespoons vegetable oil; tilt wok to coat side. Add fish; fry until golden brown, turning once. Reduce heat to low.

Cover and cook 10 minutes, turning after 3 minutes. Remove fish from wok.

Heat wok until very hot. Add 2 tablespoons vegetable oil; tilt wok to coat side. Add beans, green onion pieces, chilies and garlic; stir-fry 1 minute. Add broth; heat to boiling. Stir in cornstarch mixture; cook and stir until thickened. Add fish, wine and sesame oil; turn fish to coat both sides. Cook 2 minutes or until fish is hot. Sprinkle with sliced green onion.

4 servings

SHRIMP WITH GARLIC SAUCE

6 dried black mushrooms
½ medium head cabbage
4 green onions (with tops)
1 medium carrot
¾ pound raw medium shrimp (in shells)
1 teaspoon cornstarch
1 teaspoon water
2 tablespoons vegetable oil
2 teaspoons finely chopped garlic
2 tablespoons vegetable oil
¼ cup chicken broth
1 tablespoon chili paste

Soak mushrooms in hot water 20 minutes or until soft; drain. Rinse in warm water; drain. Squeeze out excess moisture. Remove and discard stems; cut caps into thin strips.

Cut cabbage into 2¾-inch pieces. Cut green onions diagonally into 1-inch pieces. Cut carrot diagonally into thin slices. Place carrot in boiling water; heat to boiling. Boil 1 minute; drain. Immediately rinse in cold water; drain.

Peel shrimp. Cut shrimp lengthwise into halves; wash out vein. Pat dry with paper towels. Mix cornstarch and water.

Heat wok until very hot. Add 2 tablespoons vegetable oil; tilt wok to coat side. Add shrimp and garlic, stir-fry until shrimp are pink. Remove shrimp from wok.

Heat wok until very hot. Add 2 tablespoons vegetable oil; tilt wok to coat side. Add mushrooms and cabbage; stir-fry 1 minute. Add broth; heat to boiling. Cover and cook 1 minute. Stir in cornstarch mixture; cook and stir 30 seconds or until thickened. Add shrimp, onions, carrots and chili paste. Cook and stir 30 seconds or until shrimp are hot.

4 servings

FRIED SHRIMP WITH RED SAUCE

1 pound raw medium shrimp (in shells)
1 egg, slightly beaten
1 tablespoon cornstarch
½ teaspoon salt
½ cup all-purpose flour
½ cup water
3 tablespoons cornstarch
1 tablespoon vegetable oil
½ teaspoon salt
½ teaspoon baking soda
2 teaspoons sugar
1 teaspoon cornstarch
1 teaspoon water
Vegetable oil
2 tablespoons vegetable oil
1 teaspoon finely chopped garlic
¼ cup ketchup
1 cup Chicken Broth (page 47)
2 teaspoons soy sauce
1 tablespoon chopped green onion
    (with top)

Peel shrimp. Make a shallow cut lengthwise down back of each shrimp; wash out vein. Pat dry with paper towels. Mix egg, 1 tablespoon cornstarch and ½ teaspoon salt in medium bowl; stir in shrimp. Cover and refrigerate 10 minutes.

Mix flour, ½ cup water, 3 tablespoons cornstarch, 1 tablespoon vegetable oil, ½ teaspoon salt and the baking soda in medium bowl. Stir shrimp into batter until well coated. Mix sugar, 1 teaspoon cornstarch and the water.

Heat vegetable oil (2 inches) in wok to 350°. Fry shrimp, a few at a time, 2 minutes or until light brown, turning occasionally; drain on paper towels.

Increase oil temperature to 375°. Fry shrimp all at one time 1 minute or until golden brown; drain on paper towels. Keep shrimp warm in 300° oven.

Cook and stir 2 tablespoons vegetable oil, the garlic and ketchup in 1-quart saucepan 1 minute or until hot. Add broth; heat to boiling. Add cornstarch mixture and soy sauce; cook and stir 10 seconds or until thickened. Pour sauce over shrimp; sprinkle with green onion.

4 servings

KUNG PAO SHRIMP

Roasted Peanuts (right)
1 pound raw medium shrimp (in shells)
1 teaspoon cornstarch
½ teaspoon salt
¼ teaspoon white pepper
1 medium onion
1 large green bell pepper
1 teaspoon cornstarch
1 teaspoon cold water
1 tablespoon dry white wine
½ teaspoon sugar
¼ teaspoon roasted sesame oil
3 tablespoons vegetable oil
2 teaspoons finely chopped garlic
1 teaspoon finely chopped gingerroot
2 tablespoons Hoisin sauce
2 teaspoons chili paste
2 tablespoons chopped green onions
    (with tops)

Prepare Roasted Peanuts. Peel shrimp. Make a shallow cut lengthwise down back of each shrimp; wash out vein. Pat dry with paper towels. (If shrimp are large, cut into ¾-inch pieces.) Toss shrimp, 1 teaspoon cornstarch, the salt and white pepper in medium bowl. Cover and refrigerate 30 minutes.

Cut onion into eight pieces. Cut bell pepper into ¾-inch pieces. Mix 1 teaspoon cornstarch, the water, wine, sugar and sesame oil.

Heat wok until very hot. Add vegetable oil; tilt wok to coat side. Add onion pieces, garlic and gingerroot; stir-fry 1 minute or until onion pieces are light brown. Add shrimp; stir-fry until pink. Add Hoisin sauce and chili paste; stir-fry 30 seconds. Add bell pepper; stir-fry 1 minute. Stir in cornstarch mixture; cook and stir until thickened. Sprinkle with peanuts and green onions.

4 servings

Roasted Peanuts

1 cup vegetable oil
½ cup skinless raw peanuts
Salt

Heat oil in wok to 350°. Fry peanuts until light brown. Remove from wok; drain on paper towels. Sprinkle lightly with salt.

Instead of roasting nuts as most Westerners do, Chinese cooks usually fry them until light brown. It's a quick and easy process that doesn't dry out the nut meat.

SHRIMP WITH LOBSTER SAUCE

1 pound raw medium shrimp (in shells)
1 teaspoon cornstarch
¼ teaspoon salt
¼ teaspoon roasted sesame oil
¼ cup chicken broth
1 tablespoon cornstarch
1 teaspoon dark soy sauce
1 tablespoon vegetable oil
2 tablespoons vegetable oil
½ pound lean ground pork
2 cloves garlic, finely chopped
1 teaspoon finely chopped gingerroot
½ cup Chicken Broth (page 47)
2 tablespoons dry white wine
2 eggs, slightly beaten
2 green onions (with tops), chopped

Peel shrimp. Make a shallow cut lengthwise down back of each shrimp; wash out vein. Pat dry with paper towels. Toss shrimp, 1 teaspoon cornstarch, the salt and sesame oil in medium bowl. Cover and refrigerate 30 minutes. Mix ¼ cup broth, 1 tablespoon cornstarch and the soy sauce.

Heat wok until very hot. Add 1 tablespoon vegetable oil; tilt wok to coat side. Add shrimp; stir-fry 3 minutes or until pink. Remove shrimp from wok.

Heat wok until very hot. Add 2 tablespoons vegetable oil; tilt wok to coat side. Add pork, garlic and gingerroot; stir-fry 1 minute. Add ½ cup broth and wine; heat to boiling. Stir in cornstarch mixture; heat to boiling. Gradually pour in eggs over high heat, stirring constantly so eggs form threads. Remove from heat; stir in shrimp. Sprinkle with green onions.

4 servings

Don't look for any lobster tidbits in this sauce; the name simply means that it is the same flavorful pork, garlic and ginger sauce used with Cantonese lobster.

EMPEROR'S SHRIMP

1 head iceberg lettuce
2 green onions (with tops)
1 tablespoon cornstarch
1 tablespoon water
1 pound raw medium shrimp (in shells)
2 teaspoons salt
2 tablespoons vegetable oil
1 tablespoon finely chopped garlic
¼ cup ketchup
2 teaspoons light soy sauce
½ cup Chicken Broth (page 47)
1 tablespoon dry white wine
1 teaspoon roasted sesame oil

Remove outer leaves from lettuce until head is about 4 inches in diameter. Remove core; cut 1-inch slice from core end of lettuce and discard. Place lettuce, cut side up, on round serving plate. Cut green onions into 2-inch pieces; shred lengthwise into fine strips. Cover with iced water; let stand 10 minutes or until strips curl. Mix cornstarch and water. Wash shrimp; pat dry with paper towels.

Heat wok until very hot. Add vegetable oil; tilt wok to coat side. Add shrimp and garlic; stir-fry 2 minutes or until shrimp are pink, turning once. Remove shrimp and oil from wok. Cool shrimp slightly. Remove shells and vein, leaving tails intact.

Add ketchup and soy sauce to wok; cook 30 seconds. Add broth; heat to boiling. Stir in cornstarch mixture, wine, salt and sesame oil; cook and stir until thickened. Add shrimp; heat, until all sauce coats shrimp, stirring constantly. Hang shrimp, using wooden picks, tails down, around edges of lettuce; place green onions in center.

4 servings

Emperor's Shrimp

STIR-FRIED SHRIMP WITH VEGETABLES

1 pound raw medium shrimp (in shells)
1 teaspoon cornstarch
½ teaspoon salt
½ teaspoon roasted sesame oil
⅛ teaspoon white pepper
7 large stalks bok choy
6 ounces Chinese pea pods
4 ounces mushrooms
2 green onions (with tops)
2 tablespoons oyster sauce or 1 tablespoon
    dark soy sauce
1 tablespoon cornstarch
1 tablespoon cold water
2 tablespoons vegetable oil
1 teaspoon finely chopped gingerroot
1 teaspoon finely chopped garlic
1 tablespoon vegetable oil
½ teaspoon salt
½ cup Chicken Broth (page 47)

Peel shrimp. Make a shallow cut lengthwise down back of each shrimp; wash out vein. Pat dry with paper towels. Toss shrimp, 1 teaspoon cornstarch, ½ teaspoon salt, the sesame oil and white pepper in medium bowl. Cover and refrigerate 20 minutes.

Remove leaves from bok choy stalks. Cut leaves into 2-inch pieces; cut stalks diagonally into ¼-inch slices (do not combine leaves and stalks). Remove strings from pea pods. Place pea pods in boiling water. Cover and cook 1 minute; drain. Immediately rinse in cold water; drain. Cut mushrooms into ½-inch slices. Cut green onions into 2-inch pieces; shred lengthwise into fine strips. Cover with iced water; let stand 10 minutes or until strips curl. Mix oyster sauce, 1 tablespoon cornstarch and the water.

Heat wok until very hot. Add 2 tablespoons vegetable oil; tilt wok to coat side. Add shrimp, gingerroot and garlic; stir-fry until shrimp are pink. Remove from wok.

Heat wok until very hot. Add 1 tablespoon vegetable oil; tilt wok to coat side. Add bok choy stalks, mushrooms and ½ teaspoon salt; stir-fry 1 minute. Add bok choy leaves and broth; heat to boiling. Stir in cornstarch mixture; cook and stir until thickened. Add shrimp and pea pods; cook and stir 1 minute or until shrimp are hot. Garnish with green onions.

4 servings

 Chinese cooks never boil shrimp because they believe it makes the shrimp tough and tasteless. They prefer to stir-fry shrimp, in this case, after tossing with cornstarch and sesame oil.

SHRIMP ALMOND DING

1 pound raw medium shrimp (in shells)
1 teaspoon cornstarch
½ teaspoon salt
½ teaspoon soy sauce
¼ teaspoon roasted sesame oil
3 stalks celery
½ cup sliced canned bamboo shoots
½ cup whole water chestnuts
1 medium onion
2 tablespoons cornstarch
2 tablespoons cold water
2 tablespoons vegetable oil
½ cup blanched almonds
⅛ teaspoon salt
1 teaspoon finely chopped garlic
2 tablespoons vegetable oil
1 teaspoon salt
1 can (4 ounces) button mushrooms, drained
½ cup Chicken Broth (page 47)
1 tablespoon dry white wine
½ cup frozen peas
2 tablespoons oyster sauce
2 green onions (with tops), chopped

Peel shrimp. Cut shrimp lengthwise into halves; wash out vein. Toss shrimp, 1 teaspoon cornstarch, ½ teaspoon salt, the soy sauce and sesame oil in medium bowl. Cover and refrigerate 20 minutes.

Cut celery, bamboo shoots and water chestnuts into ½-inch pieces. Cut onion into 18 pieces. Mix 2 tablespoons cornstarch and the water.

Heat wok until very hot. Add 2 tablespoons vegetable oil; tilt wok to coat side. Add almonds; stir-fry 1 minute or until light brown. Remove almonds from wok; drain on paper towel. Sprinkle with ⅛ teaspoon salt.

Heat wok until very hot. Add onion pieces and garlic; stir-fry until onion is tender. Add shrimp; stir-fry until shrimp are pink. Remove onion and shrimp from wok.

Heat wok until very hot. Add 2 tablespoons vegetable oil; tilt wok to coat side. Add celery and 1 teaspoon salt; stir-fry 1 minute. Add bamboo shoots, water chestnuts and mushrooms; stir-fry 1 minute. Stir in broth and wine; heat to boiling. Stir in cornstarch mixture; cook and stir 10 seconds or until thickened. Stir in shrimp, onion pieces, peas and oyster sauce; heat to boiling. Garnish with almonds and green onions.

5 servings

In China, almonds are considered to be good for your health and so they are added to many and various dishes. Here blanched almonds are briefly stir-fried until light brown (they will darken as they cool). Almonds add texture and flavor to recipes with lots of vegetables.

SCALLOPS WITH PEA PODS

1 pound sea scallops
½ teaspoon cornstarch
¼ teaspoon salt
⅛ teaspoon white pepper
⅛ teaspoon sesame oil
8 ounces Chinese pea pods
2 green onions (with tops)
2 tablespoons oyster sauce or 1 tablespoon
   dark soy sauce
2 tablespoons water
1 tablespoon cornstarch
3 tablespoons vegetable oil
1 teaspoon finely chopped gingerroot
1 clove garlic, finely chopped
2 tablespoons vegetable oil
½ cup sliced canned bamboo shoots or water
   chestnuts
¼ cup chicken broth

Rinse scallops in cold water 3 or 4 times; drain thoroughly. Pat dry with paper towels. Toss scallops, ½ teaspoon cornstarch, the salt, white pepper and sesame oil in medium bowl. Cover and refrigerate 30 minutes.

Remove strings from pea pods. Place pea pods in boiling water. Cover and cook 1 minute; drain. Immediately rinse in cold water; drain. Cut green onions diagonally into 2-inch pieces. Mix oyster sauce, water and 1 tablespoon cornstarch.

Heat wok until very hot. Add 3 tablespoons vegetable oil; tilt wok to coat side. Add scallops, gingerroot and garlic; stir-fry until scallops are white. Remove scallops from wok. Wash and thoroughly dry wok.

Heat wok until very hot. Add 2 tablespoons vegetable oil; tilt wok to coat side. Add bamboo shoots, stir-fry 1 minute. Add broth; heat to boiling and add scallops. Stir in cornstarch

mixture; cook and stir until thickened. Add pea pods; stir-fry 30 seconds. Sprinkle with green onions.

4 servings

 Scallops should be moist and fresh-smelling when you buy them. Be careful not to overcook or scallops will become tough and stringy and will release too much liquid to achieve the desired sauce consistency. Cook just until they are opaque.

SHRIMP TOFU CAKE

¾ pound raw medium shrimp (in shells)
14 ounces firm tofu
¼ cup chopped green onions
2 tablespoons cornstarch
2 tablespoons vegetable oil
1 teaspoon salt
1 teaspoon roasted sesame oil
¼ teaspoon white pepper
1 egg, slightly beaten
Lettuce leaves
2 tablespoons oyster sauce

Heat oven to 375°. Peel shrimp. Make a shallow cut lengthwise down back of each shrimp; wash out vein. Pat dry with paper towels. Chop shrimp.

Mash tofu with fork in medium bowl. Stir in shrimp, green onions, cornstarch, vegetable oil, salt, sesame oil, white pepper and egg with fork until well mixed. Spread shrimp mixture in greased square pan, 9 × 9 × 2 inches. Bake 25 minutes.

Line serving platter with lettuce leaves. Cut tofu cake into 3-inch squares; place on lettuce leaves. Sprinkle with oyster sauce.

6 servings

Scallops with Pea Pods and Shrimp Tofu Cake

STIR-FRIED CRABMEAT WITH CELERY CABBAGE

10 ounces frozen cooked crabmeat, thawed
½ pound celery cabbage
2 green onions (with tops)
1 tablespoon cornstarch
1 tablespoon water
1 teaspoon sugar
1 teaspoon roasted sesame oil
3 tablespoons vegetable oil
1 teaspoon finely chopped gingerroot
1 teaspoon finely chopped garlic
½ teaspoon salt
½ cup Chicken Broth (page 47)

Drain crabmeat thoroughly; remove cartilage. Squeeze out excess moisture. Cut celery cabbage into 1-inch pieces. Cut green onions diagonally into 1-inch pieces. Mix cornstarch, water, sugar and sesame oil.

Heat wok until very hot. Add vegetable oil; tilt wok to coat side. Add gingerroot and garlic; stir-fry 30 seconds. Add celery cabbage and salt; stir-fry 1 minute.

Add broth; heat to boiling. Cover and cook 2 minutes over high heat. Stir in cornstarch mixture; cook and stir until thickened. Stir in crabmeat and green onions; cook and stir 1 minute or until crabmeat is hot.

4 servings

VELVET CRABMEAT

1½ pounds broccoli
8 ounces frozen cooked crabmeat, thawed
8 egg whites
¼ cup milk
½ teaspoon salt
⅛ teaspoon white pepper
1 teaspoon sweet white wine
1 teaspoon light soy sauce
1 teaspoon roasted sesame oil
1 tablespoon vegetable oil
½ teaspoon salt
3 tablespoons vegetable oil
1 teaspoon finely chopped garlic

Pare outer layer from broccoli stalks. Cut broccoli lengthwise into 1-inch stems; remove flowerets. Cut stems diagonally into ¼-inch slices. Place broccoli in boiling water; heat to boiling. Cook uncovered 1 minute; drain. Immediately rinse in cold water; drain. Drain crabmeat thoroughly; remove cartilage. Squeeze out excess moisture.

Beat egg whites, milk, ½ teaspoon salt and the white pepper until foamy. Mix wine, soy sauce and sesame oil.

Heat wok until very hot. Add 1 tablespoon vegetable oil; tilt wok to coat side. Add broccoli and ½ teaspoon salt; stir-fry 1 minute. Remove broccoli from wok; place on heatproof platter. Keep warm in 175° oven. Wash and thoroughly dry wok.

Heat wok until very hot. Add 3 tablespoons vegetable oil to wok; do not tilt wok to coat side. Add garlic and egg white mixture; stir-fry 10 seconds. (Egg whites should not be firm before adding crabmeat.) Add crabmeat and wine mixture; cook and stir about 2 minutes or until egg white mixture is firm (do not overcook). Pour crabmeat mixture over broccoli.

Stir-fried Crabmeat with Celery Cabbage

4 servings

STIR-FRIED BROCCOLI WITH CRABMEAT

1 pound broccoli
2 cups frozen cooked crabmeat, thawed
2 green onions (with tops)
1 tablespoon cornstarch
1 tablespoon water
3 tablespoons vegetable oil
1 clove garlic, finely chopped
¼ cup chicken broth
½ teaspoon salt
½ teaspoon roasted sesame oil

Pare outer layer from broccoli stalks. Cut broccoli lengthwise into 1-inch stems; remove flowerets. Cut stems diagonally into ¼-inch slices. Place broccoli stems in boiling water; heat to boiling. Cover and cook 30 seconds. Add flowerets; heat to boiling. Cover and cook 30 seconds; drain. Immediately rinse in cold water; drain. Drain crabmeat thoroughly; remove cartilage. Squeeze out excess moisture. Cut green onions diagonally into 1-inch pieces. Mix cornstarch and water.

Heat wok until very hot. Add vegetable oil; tilt wok to coat side. Add broccoli and garlic; stir-fry 1 minute. Add broth and salt; heat to boiling. Stir in cornstarch mixture; cook and stir until thickened. Stir in crabmeat, green onions and sesame oil; cook and stir 1 minute or until crabmeat is hot.

4 servings

Fresh crabmeat adds such a wonderful flavor that the cooking and picking process is truly worth the effort. Drop 2 Dungeness crabs into boiling water in a large kettle or stockpot. Simmer about 10 minutes and drain. When crabs are cool enough to handle, break off claws and extract meat with a small fork or pick. Pull off the top shell and break off the legs. Scrape away the gills and remove internal organs carefully. Pick out as much meat as you can find in the body and legs.

CLAMS WITH SALTED BLACK BEANS AND CHILIES

2 tablespoons salted black beans
2 hot green chilies
1 tablespoon cornstarch
1 teaspoon sugar
1 tablespoon water
36 clams
3 cups cold water
3 tablespoons vinegar
½ cup boiling water
3 tablespoons vegetable oil
2 teaspoons finely chopped garlic
1 teaspoon finely chopped gingerroot
1 green onion (with top), chopped

Place beans in small bowl; cover with warm water. Stir beans about 2 minutes to remove excess salt. Remove beans from water; drain well. Remove seeds and membranes from chilies. Cut chilies into very thin slices. Mix cornstarch, sugar and 1 tablespoon water.

Discard any broken or open clams; place remaining clams in a large bowl. Mix 3 cups water and the vinegar; pour over clams. Let stand 30 minutes. Scrub clams under running cold water.

Place clams in steamer with ½ cup boiling water. (If steamer is not available, place clams in Dutch oven. Add 1 inch boiling water and cover tightly.) Steam 5 minutes or until clams open at least 1 inch; remove clams as they open. (Discard clams that do not open.) Strain clam liquid through double-thickness cheesecloth; reserve 1 cup. Remove clams from shells; cut each clam into halves. Keep clams warm.

Heat wok until very hot. Add vegetable oil; tilt to coat side. Add beans, chilies, garlic and gingerroot; stir-fry 1 minute.

Add reserved liquid; heat to boiling. Stir in cornstarch mixture; cook and stir 1 minute or until thickened. Pour bean mixture over clams; sprinkle with chopped green onion.

4 servings

Fresh clams are a must here; their delicate scent of the sea blends beautifully with garlic, ginger and hot green chilies. Discard any clams that are open before cooking and any that don't open when steamed. Be careful when handling chilies; the seeds and ribs are especially hot and can actually burn your skin. Rubber gloves are a good idea, and, whatever you do, avoid touching your eyes or lips after you have handled hot peppers.

CLAMS WITH WHITE RADISHES

2 tablespoons salted black beans
¾ pound white radishes
2 green onions (with tops)
2 tablespoons cornstarch
2 tablespoons water
1 teaspoon sugar
1 teaspoon light soy sauce
24 clams
3 cups cold water
3 tablespoons vinegar
½ cup boiling water
3 tablespoons vegetable oil
2 teaspoons finely chopped garlic
2 teaspoons finely chopped gingerroot

Place beans in small bowl; cover with warm water. Stir beans about 2 minutes to remove excess salt. Remove beans from water; drain well. Cut radishes diagonally into ¼-inch slices. Cut green onions diagonally into 2-inch pieces. Mix cornstarch, 2 tablespoons water, the sugar and soy sauce.

Discard any broken or open clams; place remaining clams in large bowl. Mix 3 cups water and the vinegar; pour over clams. Let stand 30 minutes. Scrub clams under running cold water.

Place clams in steamer with ½ cup boiling water. (If steamer is not available, place clams in Dutch oven. Add 1 inch boiling water and cover tightly.) Steam clams 5 to 6 minutes or until clams open at least 1 inch; remove clams as they open. (Discard clams that do not open.) Strain clam liquid through double-thickness cheesecloth; reserve ½ cup. Remove clams from shells; cut each clam into halves. Keep clams warm.

Heat wok until very hot. Add vegetable oil; tilt wok to coat side. Add beans, garlic and gingerroot; stir-fry 10 seconds. Add radishes and reserved liquid; reduce heat to medium. Cover and cook 5 minutes. Stir in cornstarch mixture; cook and stir until thickened. Add green onions and clams; stir-fry 1 minute.

4 servings

5

肉

MEATS

SWEET-AND-SOUR PORK

1½-pound pork boneless loin or leg
1 egg, slightly beaten
2 tablespoons cornstarch
2 tablespoons vegetable oil
1 teaspoon salt
1 teaspoon light soy sauce
¼ teaspoon white pepper
2 tomatoes
1 green bell pepper
Vegetable oil
¾ cup all-purpose flour
¾ cup water
2 tablespoons cornstarch
1 teaspoon salt
1 teaspoon baking soda
1 cup plus 2 tablespoons sugar
1 cup Chicken Broth (page 47)
¾ cup white vinegar
1 tablespoon vegetable oil
2 teaspoons dark soy sauce
1 teaspoon salt
1 clove garlic, finely chopped
¼ cup cornstarch
¼ cup cold water
1 can (8¼ ounces) pineapple chunks, drained

Trim fat from pork; cut pork into ¾-inch pieces. Mix egg, 2 tablespoons cornstarch, 2 tablespoons vegetable oil, 1 teaspoon salt, 1 teaspoon soy sauce and the white pepper in medium bowl; stir in pork. Cover and refrigerate 20 minutes.

Cut each tomato into 8 wedges. Cut bell pepper into 1-inch pieces.

Heat vegetable oil (1½ inches) in wok to 350°. Mix flour, ¾ cup water, 2 tablespoons cornstarch, 1 teaspoon salt and the baking soda in medium bowl. Stir pork pieces into batter until well coated. Fry about 15 pieces at a time 4 minutes or until light brown, turning frequently; drain on paper towels. Increase oil temperature to 375°. Fry pork all at one time 1 minute or until golden brown; drain on paper towels. Place pork on heated platter.

Heat sugar, broth, vinegar, 1 tablespoon vegetable oil, 2 teaspoons soy sauce, 1 teaspoon salt and the garlic to boiling in 3-quart saucepan. Mix ¼ cup cornstarch and ¼ cup water; stir into sauce. Cook and stir about 20 seconds or until thickened. Stir in tomatoes, bell pepper and pineapple. Heat to boiling; pour over pork.

8 servings

Sweet-and-Sour Pork

87

MOU SHU PORK

Mandarin Pancakes (right)
1¼-pound pork boneless loin or leg
1 teaspoon cornstarch
1 teaspoon salt
1 teaspoon light soy sauce
½ teaspoon sugar
½ teaspoon white pepper
6 large dried black mushrooms
2 green onions (with tops)
1 can (8½ ounces) sliced bamboo shoots, drained
2 tablespoons cold water
1 teaspoon cornstarch
1 teaspoon soy sauce
2 tablespoons vegetable oil
1 egg, slightly beaten
¼ teaspoon salt
Dash of white pepper
2 tablespoons vegetable oil
1 teaspoon finely chopped garlic
¼ cup chicken broth

Prepare Mandarin Pancakes. Trim fat from pork loin; cut pork with grain into 2 × 1-inch strips. Cut strips across grain into ⅛-inch slices. Stack slices; cut into thin strips. Toss pork, 1 teaspoon cornstarch, 1 teaspoon salt, 1 teaspoon soy sauce, the sugar and ½ teaspoon white pepper in medium bowl. Cover and refrigerate 30 minutes.

Soak mushrooms in hot water 20 minutes or until soft; drain. Rinse in warm water; drain. Squeeze out excess moisture. Remove and discard stems; cut caps into thin strips. Cut green onions diagonally into 2-inch pieces. Cut bamboo shoots lengthwise into thin strips. Mix water, 1 teaspoon cornstarch and 1 teaspoon soy sauce.

Heat wok until very hot. Add 2 tablespoons vegetable oil; tilt wok to coat side. Mix egg, ¼ teaspoon salt and dash of white pepper; pour into wok. Tilt wok to coat bottom with egg, forming a thin pancake. Fry egg 10 seconds or until firm, turning once. Remove egg from wok; cut into thin strips.

Heat wok until very hot. Add 2 tablespoons vegetable oil to wok; tilt to coat side. Add garlic; stir-fry until brown. Add pork; stir-fry 2 minutes until pork is no longer pink. Add mushrooms and bamboo shoots; stir-fry 1 minute. Stir in broth; cook and stir 2 minutes. Stir in cornstarch mixture; cook and stir 10 seconds or until thickened. Add green onions and egg strips; cook and stir 30 seconds.

To serve, spoon about ¼ cup pork mixture onto the center of each pancake. Fold two opposite sides over filling, overlapping edges about ½ inch in center. Fold one unfolded edge over folded sides to form a pocket. Serve with Hoisin sauce if desired.

8 servings

Mandarin Pancakes

2¼ cups all-purpose flour
1 cup boiling water
Sesame oil

Mix flour and water with fork until dough holds together. Turn dough onto lightly floured surface; knead about 8 minutes or until smooth. Shape dough into 8-inch roll; cut roll into eight 1-inch slices. Cut each slice into halves. (Cover pieces of dough with plastic wrap to keep them from drying out.)

Shape each of 2 pieces of dough into a ball; flatten slightly. Roll each ball of dough into a 4-inch circle on lightly floured surface. Brush top of 1 circle with sesame oil; top with remaining circle. Roll each double circle into a

7-inch circle on lightly floured surface (see illustration). Repeat with remaining pieces of dough. (Cover circles with plastic wrap to keep them from drying out.)

Heat 8- or 9-inch ungreased skillet over medium heat until warm. Cook one double circle at a time, turning frequently, just until pancake is blistered with air pockets, turns slightly translucent and feels dry. (Do not overcook or pancake will become brittle.) Carefully separate into 2 pancakes; loosely fold each pancake into fourths. Repeat each step with remaining circles.

Heat pancakes before serving. Place folded pancakes on heatproof plate or rack in steamer; cover and steam over boiling water 10 minutes. (Add boiling water if necessary.)

Brush circle with sesame oil; top with another circle.

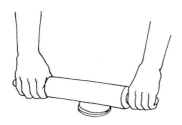

Roll double circle into a 7-inch circle.

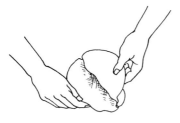

After frying, carefully separate into 2 pancakes; fold each pancake loosely into fourths.

Of the countless Chinese dishes that include shredded pork, Mou Shu Pork is probably the most intriguing. At the table, diners fill Mandarin pancakes with flavorful, stir-fried pork, green onions and bamboo shoots and then fold them into a Far East version of burritos. Mandarin pancakes take a little practice to perfect, but they are worth the trouble. Be creative and substitute various meats and vegetables, always thinly shredded. Make pancakes ahead of time, if you choose; cover and refrigerate for 1 day or freeze for up to 2 months. Don't reheat the pancakes in the microwave as they'll get dry. They should be steamed.

SHREDDED PORK WITH GREEN ONIONS

1-pound pork boneless loin or leg
1 teaspoon salt
1 teaspoon cornstarch
1 teaspoon light soy sauce
4 green onions (with tops)
2 teaspoons sugar
2 tablespoons dry white wine
2 tablespoons dark soy sauce
2 tablespoons vegetable oil
2 teaspoons finely chopped garlic

Trim fat from pork loin; cut pork with grain into 2 × 1-inch strips. Cut strips across grain into 1/8-inch slices. Stack slices; cut into thin strips. Toss pork, salt, cornstarch and 1 teaspoon soy sauce in medium bowl. Cover and refrigerate 30 minutes.

Cut green onions diagonally into 1-inch pieces. Mix sugar, wine and 2 tablespoons soy sauce.

Heat wok until very hot. Add vegetable oil; tilt wok to coat side. Add pork; stir-fry 2 minutes or until pork is no longer pink. Add garlic; stir-fry 10 seconds. Add green onions and soy sauce mixture; stir-fry 1 minute.

4 servings

PORK WITH STRAW MUSHROOMS

1¼-pound pork boneless loin or leg
2 teaspoons cornstarch
1 teaspoon salt
1 teaspoon soy sauce
½ teaspoon sugar
Dash of white pepper
8 ounces Chinese pea pods
3 green onions (with tops)
1 tablespoon cornstarch
1 tablespoon cold water
2 tablespoons vegetable oil
1 teaspoon finely chopped garlic
2 cans (8 ounces each) straw mushrooms, drained
1 can (8½ ounces) sliced bamboo shoots, drained
1 tablespoon dark soy sauce
¼ cup chicken broth

Trim fat from pork loin; cut pork with grain into 2 × 1-inch strips. Cut strips across grain into ⅛-inch slices. Toss pork, 2 teaspoons cornstarch, the salt, 1 teaspoon soy sauce, the sugar and white pepper in medium bowl. Cover and refrigerate 20 minutes. Remove strings from pea pods. Place pea pods in boiling water. Cover and cook 1 minute; drain. Immediately rinse in cold water; drain. Cut green onions diagonally into 2-inch pieces. Mix 1 tablespoon cornstarch and the water.

Heat wok until very hot. Add vegetable oil; tilt wok to coat side. Add pork and garlic; stir-fry 2 minutes or until pork is no longer pink. Add mushrooms, bamboo shoots and dark soy sauce; stir-fry 1 minute. Stir in broth; heat to boiling. Stir in cornstarch mixture; cook and stir until thickened. Add green onions and pea pods; cook and stir 30 seconds.

6 servings

Mou Shu Pork (page 88)

SHREDDED PORK WITH BEAN SPROUTS

1-pound pork boneless loin or leg
1 tablespoon cornstarch
½ teaspoon salt
⅛ teaspoon white pepper
6 medium dried black mushrooms
1 pound bean sprouts
4 green onions (with tops)
1 tablespoon cornstarch
1 teaspoon sugar
2 teaspoons light soy sauce
2 tablespoons vegetable oil
1 teaspoon finely chopped garlic
½ teaspoon salt
¼ cup chicken broth

Trim fat from pork loin; cut pork with grain into 2 × 1-inch strips. Cut strips across grain into ⅛-inch slices. Stack slices; cut into thin strips. Toss pork, 1 tablespoon cornstarch, ½ teaspoon salt and the white pepper in medium bowl. Cover and refrigerate 30 minutes.

Soak mushrooms in hot water 20 minutes or until soft; drain. Rinse in warm water; drain. Squeeze out excess moisture. Remove and discard stems; cut caps into ½-inch strips.

Rinse bean sprouts in cold water; drain. Cut green onions diagonally into 1-inch pieces. Mix 1 tablespoon cornstarch, the sugar and soy sauce.

Heat wok until very hot. Add 2 tablespoons vegetable oil; tilt wok to coat side. Add pork; stir-fry 2 minutes or until pork is no longer pink. Add mushrooms, garlic, and ½ teaspoon salt; stir-fry 30 seconds. Add bean sprouts and green onions; stir-fry 2 minutes. Stir in broth; heat to boiling. Stir in cornstarch mixture; cook and stir 15 seconds or until thickened.

4 servings

SICHUAN PORK

1¼-pound pork boneless loin or leg
2 teaspoons cornstarch
½ teaspoon salt
½ teaspoon sugar
¼ teaspoon white pepper
2 green onions (with tops)
1 small green bell pepper
1 small red bell pepper
1 can (8½ ounces) sliced bamboo shoots,
     drained
2 tablespoons vegetable oil
2 teaspoons finely chopped garlic
1 teaspoon finely chopped gingerroot
2 teaspoons chili paste

Trim fat from pork loin; cut pork with grain
into 2 × 1-inch strips. Cut strips across grain
into ⅛-inch slices. Stack slices; cut into thin
strips. Toss pork, cornstarch, salt, sugar and
white pepper in medium bowl. Cover and
refrigerate 30 minutes.

Cut green onions diagonally into 2-inch pieces.
Cut bell peppers into ⅛-inch strips. Cut bamboo shoots lengthwise into thin strips.

Heat wok until very hot. Add vegetable oil;
tilt wok to coat side. Add pork, garlic and
gingerroot; stir-fry 2 minutes or until pork is
no longer pink. Add bell peppers and bamboo shoots; stir-fry 1 minute. Stir in green
onions and chili paste.

4 servings

STIR-FRIED PORK WITH SALTED BLACK BEANS

1-pound pork boneless loin or leg
½ teaspoon salt
⅛ teaspoon white pepper
1 tablespoon cornstarch
¼ cup salted black beans
5 stalks celery
2 green onions (with tops)
1 tablespoon cornstarch
1 teaspoon sugar
1 tablespoon cold water
3 tablespoons vegetable oil
2 tablespoons vegetable oil
2 teaspoons finely chopped garlic
½ cup Chicken Broth (page 47)

Trim fat from pork loin; cut pork with grain
into 2 × 1-inch strips. Cut strips across grain
into ⅛-inch slices. Toss pork, salt and white
pepper in medium bowl. Let stand 10 minutes; toss with 1 tablespoon cornstarch. Cover
and refrigerate 30 minutes.

Place beans in bowl; cover with warm water.
Stir beans about 2 minutes to remove excess
salt. Remove beans from water; drain well.
Cut celery diagonally into ¼-inch slices. Cut
green onions diagonally into 1-inch pieces.
Mix 1 tablespoon cornstarch, the sugar and
water.

Heat wok until very hot. Add 3 tablespoons
vegetable oil; tilt wok to coat side. Add pork;
stir-fry 2 minutes or until pork is no longer
pink. Remove pork from wok.

Add 2 tablespoons vegetable oil; the beans,
celery and garlic; stir-fry 30 seconds. Add
broth; cover and heat to boiling. Stir in cornstarch mixture; cook and stir 15 seconds or
until thickened. Add pork and green onions;
cook and stir 1 minute.

4 servings

SESAME PORK

1¼-pound pork boneless loin
1 egg, slightly beaten
2 tablespoons cornstarch
2 tablespoons vegetable oil
1 teaspoon salt
1 teaspoon light soy sauce
¼ teaspoon white pepper
2 tablespoons cornstarch
2 tablespoons water
2 tablespoons vegetable oil
2 teaspoons dried ground chili
2 teaspoons finely chopped garlic
1 teaspoon finely chopped gingerroot
¾ cup sugar
¾ cup Chicken Broth (page 47)
⅔ cup vinegar
2 teaspoons dark soy sauce
Vegetable oil
2 ounces rice stick noodles
¾ cup all-purpose flour
¾ cup water
3 tablespoons cornstarch
1 tablespoon salt
1 teaspoon baking soda
3 tablespoons Toasted Sesame Seed (page 34)
2 tablespoons chopped green onion
    (with tops)

Trim fat from pork loin; cut pork into ¾-inch pieces. Mix egg, 2 tablespoons cornstarch, 2 tablespoons vegetable oil, 1 teaspoon salt, 1 teaspoon light soy sauce and the white pepper in medium bowl; stir in pork. Cover and refrigerate 30 minutes.

Mix 2 tablespoons cornstarch and 2 tablespoons water. Heat 2 tablespoons vegetable oil over medium heat in 2-quart saucepan; reduce heat to low. Add chili, garlic, and gingerroot; cook 30 seconds. Add sugar, broth, vinegar and 2 teaspoons dark soy sauce; heat to boiling. Add cornstarch mixture; cook and stir 15 seconds or until thickened. Keep sauce warm.

Heat vegetable oil (1 inch) in wok to 425°. Fry noodles, ¼ at a time 5 seconds or until puffed, turning once; drain on paper towels.

Reduce oil temperature to 350°. Mix flour, ¾ cup water, 3 tablespoons cornstarch, 1 tablespoon salt and the baking soda. Stir pork into batter until pork is well coated. Fry 15 to 18 pieces of pork at a time 4 minutes or until light brown, turning occasionally; drain on paper towels.

Increase oil temperature to 375°. Fry pork all at one time 1 minute or until golden brown; drain on paper towels. Place noodles on heated platter. Mix pork with sauce; pour over noodles. Sprinkle with sesame seed and green onions.

4 to 6 servings

Texture is almost as important as flavor in this dish. Frying the meat twice gives it an exceptionally crisp exterior and a rich, deep color. The puffed, crunchy rice noodles are a perfect complement.

SPARERIBS WITH SALTED BLACK BEANS

1½-pound rack pork ribs, cut across bones
    into halves
1 teaspoon sugar
2 teaspoons light soy sauce
1 egg
3 tablespoons cornstarch
2 tablespoons salted black beans
4 green onions (with tops)
1 green bell pepper
2 tablespoons cornstarch
½ cup Chicken Broth (page 47)
1 teaspoon sugar
2 teaspoons dark soy sauce
Vegetable oil
2 teaspoons finely chopped garlic
2 teaspoons finely chopped gingerroot
½ cup Chicken Broth (page 47)

Trim fat and remove membranes from pork ribs; cut between each rib to separate. Mix 1 teaspoon sugar, 2 teaspoons light soy sauce and the egg in large bowl; stir in ribs. Let stand 10 minutes; toss with 3 tablespoons cornstarch. Cover and refrigerate 20 minutes.

Place beans in bowl; cover with warm water. Stir beans about 2 minutes to remove excess salt. Remove beans from water; drain well.

Cut green onions diagonally into 1-inch pieces. Cut bell pepper into 1-inch squares. Mix 2 tablespoons cornstarch, ½ cup broth, 1 teaspoon sugar and 2 teaspoons dark soy sauce.

Heat vegetable oil (1½ inches) in wok to 350°. Fry ribs, six or seven at a time, 5 minutes or until golden brown. Remove ribs; drain oil from wok, reserving 3 tablespoons.

Heat wok until very hot. Add 3 tablespoons reserved vegetable oil; tilt wok to coat side. Add garlic, gingerroot and beans; stir-fry 15 seconds. Add ribs, green onions, bell pepper and ½ cup broth. Cover and cook 2 minutes. Stir in cornstarch mixture; cook and stir 15 seconds or until thickened.

4 servings

SHREDDED PORK WITH SWEET-AND-SOUR SAUCE

1-pound pork boneless loin or leg
1 tablespoon cornstarch
½ teaspoon salt
⅛ teaspoon white pepper
1 green bell pepper
1 red bell pepper
2 tablespoons sugar
1 tablespoon cornstarch
2 tablespoons white vinegar
1 tablespoon dark soy sauce
2 tablespoons vegetable oil
2 teaspoons finely chopped garlic
1 teaspoon finely chopped gingerroot

Trim fat from pork loin; cut pork with grain into 2 × 1-inch strips. Cut strips across grain into ⅛-inch slices. Stack slices; cut into thin strips. Toss pork, 1 tablespoon cornstarch, the salt and white pepper in medium bowl. Cover and refrigerate 30 minutes.

Cut bell peppers into ⅛-inch strips. Mix sugar, 1 tablespoon cornstarch, the vinegar and soy sauce.

Heat wok until very hot. Add vegetable oil; tilt wok to coat side. Add pork, garlic and gingerroot; stir-fry 2 minutes or until pork is no longer pink. Add bell peppers; stir-fry 15 seconds. Stir in cornstarch mixture; cook and stir 15 seconds or until thickened.

4 or 5 servings

Spareribs with Salted Black Beans

KUNG PAO PORK

1 cup Roasted Peanuts (page 75)
1-pound pork boneless loin or leg
2 teaspoons cornstarch
½ teaspoon salt
⅛ teaspoon white pepper
1 small red bell pepper
4 green onions (with tops)
1 tablespoon cornstarch
1 teaspoon sugar
¼ cup chicken broth
2 tablespoons vegetable oil
2 teaspoons finely chopped garlic
2 tablespoons chili paste

Prepare Roasted Peanuts. Trim fat from pork loin; cut pork into ¾-inch pieces. Toss pork, 2 teaspoons cornstarch, the salt and white pepper in medium bowl. Cover and refrigerate 30 minutes.

Cut bell pepper into ¾-inch squares. Cut green onions diagonally into ¾-inch pieces. Mix 1 tablespoon cornstarch, the sugar and broth.

Heat wok until very hot. Add vegetable oil; tilt wok to coat side. Add pork; stir-fry 2 minutes or until pork is no longer pink. Add green onions, garlic and chili paste; stir-fry 20 seconds. Add bell pepper; stir-fry 2 minutes. Stir in cornstarch mixture; cook and stir 15 seconds or until thickened. Sprinkle with peanuts.

4 servings

Anything with "Kung Pao" is spiced with chili paste and garlic and stir-fried with peanuts. The classic Sichuan flavors work as well with chicken, shrimp and beef as they do with pork. Kung Pao is rich tasting. Adjust the spiciness to your taste.

BEEF WITH SALTED BLACK BEANS AND PEPPERS

1-pound beef flank or boneless sirloin steak
1 tablespoon vegetable oil
1 teaspoon cornstarch
½ teaspoon salt
Dash of white pepper
3 tablespoons salted black beans
1 green bell pepper
1 red bell pepper
3 tablespoons vegetable oil
2 tablespoons vegetable oil
2 teaspoons finely chopped gingerroot
2 teaspoons finely chopped garlic.
1 teaspoon sugar

Trim fat from beef steak; cut beef with grain into 2-inch strips. Cut strips across grain into ⅛-inch slices. Toss beef, 1 tablespoon oil, the cornstarch, salt and white pepper in medium bowl. Cover and refrigerate 30 minutes.

Place beans in small bowl; cover with warm water. Stir beans about 2 minutes to remove excess salt. Remove beans from water; drain well. Cut bell peppers into ¾-inch squares.

Heat wok until very hot. Add 3 tablespoons vegetable oil; tilt wok to coat side. Add beef; stir-fry 2 minutes or until beef is brown. Remove beef from wok.

Heat wok until very hot. Add 2 tablespoons oil; tilt wok to coat side. Add beans, gingerroot and garlic; stir-fry 30 seconds. Add bell peppers, beef and sugar; stir-fry 1 minute.

4 or 5 servings

KUNG PAO BEEF

½ cup Roasted Peanuts (page 75)
1-pound beef flank or boneless sirloin steak
1 tablespoon vegetable oil
2 teaspoons cornstarch
½ teaspoon salt
Dash of white pepper
2 hot green chilies
2 green onions (with tops)
1 medium red bell pepper
2 tablespoons vegetable oil
2 tablespoons vegetable oil
2 teaspoons finely chopped garlic.
1 teaspoon finely chopped gingerroot
2 tablespoons brown bean sauce
½ cup diced canned bamboo shoots
1 teaspoon sugar

Prepare Roasted Peanuts. Trim fat from beef steak; cut beef into ¾-inch cubes. Toss beef, 1 tablespoon oil, the cornstarch, salt and white pepper in medium bowl. Cover and refrigerate 30 minutes.

Remove seeds and membranes from chilies. Cut chilies into very thin slices. Cut green onions diagonally into 1-inch pieces. Cut bell pepper into ¾-inch squares.

Heat wok until very hot. Add 2 tablespoons vegetable oil; tilt wok to coat side. Add beef; stir-fry 2 minutes or until beef is brown. Remove beef from wok.

Heat wok until very hot. Add 2 tablespoons vegetable oil, tilt wok to coat side. Add chilies, garlic, gingerroot, bean sauce and bamboo shoots; stir-fry 1 minute. Add beef, bell pepper and sugar; stir-fry 1 minute. Stir in green onions. Sprinkle with peanuts.

4 or 5 servings

BEEF AND BROCCOLI WITH GARLIC SAUCE

1-pound beef boneless sirloin or round steak
1 tablespoon vegetable oil
½ teaspoon salt
Dash of white pepper
1½ pounds broccoli
1 teaspoon cornstarch
1 teaspoon sesame oil
¼ cup chicken broth
2 tablespoons vegetable oil
1 tablespoon vegetable oil
1 tablespoon finely chopped garlic
1 teaspoon finely chopped gingerroot
2 tablespoons brown bean sauce
1 cup sliced canned bamboo shoots

Trim fat from beef steak; cut beef lengthwise into 2-inch strips. Cut strips crosswise into ⅛-inch slices. Toss beef, 1 tablespoon vegetable oil, the salt and white pepper in medium bowl. Cover and refrigerate 30 minutes.

Pare outer layer from broccoli stalks. Cut broccoli lengthwise into 1-inch stems; remove flowerets. Cut stems into 1-inch pieces. Place broccoli in boiling water; heat to boiling. Cover and cook 2 minutes; drain. Immediately rinse in cold water; drain. Mix cornstarch, sesame oil and broth.

Heat wok until very hot. Add 2 tablespoons vegetable oil; tilt wok to coat side. Add beef; stir-fry 2 minutes or until beef is brown. Remove beef from wok.

Heat wok until very hot. Add 1 tablespoon oil; tilt wok to coat side. Add garlic, gingerroot and bean sauce; stir-fry 30 seconds. Add bamboo shoots; stir-fry 1 minute. Stir in beef and broccoli. Stir in cornstarch mixture; cook and stir 15 seconds or until thickened.

4 or 5 servings

STIR-FRIED BEEF WITH EGGPLANT

½-pound beef boneless sirloin or flank steak
1 tablespoon vegetable oil
1 tablespoon finely chopped garlic
1 teaspoon cornstarch
½ teaspoon salt
Dash of white pepper
2 tablespoons salted black beans
1 large eggplant
1 teaspoon finely chopped gingerroot
4 green onions (with tops)
2 tablespoons cornstarch
2 tablespoons water
1 teaspoon sugar
1 tablespoon dark soy sauce
2 tablespoons vegetable oil
3 tablespoons vegetable oil
1½ cups Chicken Broth (page 47)

Trim fat from beef steak; cut beef lengthwise into 2-inch strips. Cut strips crosswise into ⅛-inch slices. Toss beef, 1 tablespoon vegetable oil, the garlic, 1 teaspoon cornstarch, the salt and white pepper in medium bowl. Cover and refrigerate 30 minutes.

Place beans in bowl; cover with warm water. Stir beans about 2 minutes to remove excess salt. Remove beans from water; drain well.

Pare eggplant; cut into ¼-inch pieces. Mix eggplant, beans and gingerroot. Cut green onions diagonally into 2-inch pieces. Mix 2 tablespoons cornstarch, the water, sugar and soy sauce.

Heat wok until very hot. Add 2 tablespoons vegetable oil; tilt wok to coat side. Add beef; stir-fry 2 minutes or until beef is brown. Remove beef from wok.

Heat wok until very hot. Add 3 tablespoons vegetable oil; tilt wok to coat side. Add eggplant mixture; stir-fry 1 minute. Add broth; heat to boiling. Cover and simmer 2 minutes. Add cornstarch mixture; cook and stir 20 seconds or until thickened. Add beef and green onions; cook and stir 1 minute or until beef is hot.

3 servings

STIR-FRIED BEEF WITH ASPARAGUS

1-pound beef flank or boneless sirloin steak
1 tablespoon vegetable oil
1 teaspoon cornstarch
1 teaspoon salt
1 teaspoon sugar
1 teaspoon soy sauce
Dash of white pepper
10 medium dried black mushrooms
1 pound asparagus
4 ounces Chinese pea pods
2 green onions (with tops)
¼ cup chicken broth
2 tablespoons cornstarch
2 tablespoons oyster sauce
1 teaspoon sugar
3 tablespoons vegetable oil
1 teaspoon finely chopped gingerroot
1 teaspoon finely chopped garlic
2 tablespoons vegetable oil
1 teaspoon salt
2 tablespoons dry white wine
½ cup Chicken Broth (page 47)

Trim fat from beef steak; cut beef with grain into 2-inch strips. Cut strips across grain into ⅛-inch slices. Toss beef, 1 tablespoon vegetable oil, 1 teaspoon cornstarch, 1 teaspoon salt, 1 teaspoon sugar, the soy sauce and white pepper in medium bowl. Cover and refrigerate 20 minutes.

Soak mushrooms in hot water 20 minutes or until soft; drain. Rinse in warm water; drain. Squeeze out excess moisture. Remove and discard stems; cut caps into ½-inch pieces.

Break off tough ends of asparagus where stalks snap easily. Cut asparagus diagonally into 2-inch pieces. Remove strings from pea pods. Place pea pods in boiling water. Cover and cook 1 minute; drain. Immediately rinse in cold water; drain. Cut green onions into 2-inch pieces; cut pieces lengthwise into thin strips. Mix ¼ cup broth, 2 tablespoons cornstarch, the oyster sauce and 1 teaspoon sugar.

Heat wok until very hot. Add 3 tablespoons vegetable oil; tilt wok to coat side. Add beef, gingerroot and garlic; stir-fry 2 minutes or until beef is brown. Remove beef from wok.

Heat wok until very hot. Add 2 tablespoons vegetable oil; tilt wok to coat side. Add mushrooms, asparagus and 1 teaspoon salt; stir-fry 1 minute. Add wine; stir-fry 30 seconds. Stir in ½ cup broth; heat to boiling. Stir in beef; heat to boiling. Stir in cornstarch mixture; cook and stir 20 seconds or until thickened. Add pea pods; cook and stir 30 seconds. Garnish with green onions.

5 servings

陳 *One charming aspect of Chinese cuisine is the emphasis on the aesthetic. In this dish, the beef is cut into strips that echo the long, flat shape of the pea pods; the pieces of asparagus mirror the cut-up green onions. Take care to wash the asparagus tips free of all sand and dirt.*

STIR-FRIED BEEF WITH CELERY CABBAGE

1-pound beef flank or boneless sirloin steak
2 teaspoons cornstarch
1 teaspoon finely chopped gingerroot
1 teaspoon vegetable oil
½ teaspoon salt
⅛ teaspoon white pepper
6 medium dried black mushrooms
1 pound celery cabbage
4 green onions (with tops)
1 tablespoon cornstarch
2 tablespoons beef or chicken broth
2 tablespoons vegetable oil
2 teaspoons dark soy sauce
2 tablespoons vegetable oil
1 teaspoon finely chopped garlic
½ teaspoon salt

Trim fat from beef steak; cut beef with grain into 2-inch strips. Cut strips across grain into ⅛-inch slices. Toss beef, 2 teaspoons cornstarch, gingerroot, 1 teaspoon vegetable oil, ½ teaspoon salt and the white pepper in medium bowl. Cover and refrigerate 30 minutes.

Soak mushrooms in hot water 20 minutes or until soft, drain. Squeeze out excess moisture. Remove and discard stems; cut caps into ½-inch pieces.

Cut celery cabbage diagonally into ¾-inch slices. Cut green onions diagonally into 1-inch pieces. Mix 1 tablespoon cornstarch and the broth.

Heat wok until very hot. Add 2 tablespoons vegetable oil; tilt wok to coat side. Add beef; stir-fry 2 minutes or until beef is brown. Stir in soy sauce. Remove beef from wok.

Heat wok until very hot. Add 2 tablespoons vegetable oil; tilt wok to coat side. Add celery cabbage, garlic and ½ teaspoon salt; stir-fry 2 minutes. Stir in cornstarch mixture; cook and stir 15 seconds or until thickened. Add beef and green onions; cook and stir 1 minute.

4 or 5 servings

STIR-FRIED SHREDDED BEEF WITH GREEN PEPPER

1-pound beef boneless sirloin or round steak
1 tablespoon cornstarch
2 teaspoons vegetable oil
½ teaspoon salt
¼ teaspoon white pepper
6 shallots
1 large green bell pepper
2 teaspoons cornstarch
1 teaspoon sugar
1 tablespoon water
2 teaspoons mushroom soy sauce
½ teaspoon sesame oil
3 tablespoons vegetable oil
1 teaspoon finely chopped gingerroot

Trim fat from beef steak; cut beef lengthwise into 2-inch strips. Cut strips crosswise into ¼-inch slices. Stack slices; cut lengthwise into thin strips. Toss beef, 1 tablespoon cornstarch, 2 teaspoons vegetable oil, the salt and white pepper in medium bowl. Cover and refrigerate 30 minutes.

Cut shallots into thin slices. Cut bell pepper into thin strips. Mix 2 teaspoons cornstarch, the sugar, water, soy sauce and sesame oil.

Heat wok until very hot. Add 3 tablespoons vegetable oil; tilt wok to coat side. Add beef and gingerroot; stir-fry 1 minute. Add shallots and green pepper, stir-fry 1 minute. Stir in cornstarch mixture; cook and stir 15 seconds or until thickened.

4 or 5 servings

STIR-FRIED BEEF WITH VEGETABLES

1-pound beef boneless sirloin or round steak
1 teaspoon cornstarch
½ teaspoon salt
⅛ teaspoon white pepper
1 tablespoon vegetable oil
4 large stalks bok choy
8 ounces Chinese pea pods
2 tablespoons cornstarch
½ teaspoon sugar
¼ cup water
2 tablespoons oyster sauce
2 tablespoons vegetable oil
2 tablespoons vegetable oil
1 teaspoon finely chopped gingerroot
2 cloves garlic, finely chopped
1 teaspoon salt
1 cup sliced mushrooms
½ cup sliced canned bamboo shoots
½ cup sliced water chestnuts
¾ cup Chicken Broth (page 47)
2 teaspoons dry white wine

Trim fat from beef steak; cut beef lengthwise into 2-inch strips. Cut strips crosswise into ⅛-inch slices. Toss beef, 1 teaspoon cornstarch, ½ teaspoon salt, the white pepper, and 1 tablespoon vegetable oil in medium bowl. Cover and refrigerate 30 minutes.

Remove leaves from bok choy stems. Cut leaves into 2-inch pieces; cut stems diagonally into ¼-inch slices (do not combine leaves and stems). Remove strings from pea pods. Place pea pods in boiling water. Cover and cook 1 minute; drain. Immediately rinse in cold water; drain. Mix 2 tablespoons cornstarch, the sugar, water and oyster sauce.

Heat wok until very hot. Add 2 tablespoons vegetable oil; tilt wok to coat side. Add beef; stir-fry 2 minutes or until beef is brown. Remove beef from wok.

Heat wok until very hot. Add 2 tablespoons vegetable oil; tilt to coat side. Add bok choy stems, gingerroot, garlic and 1 teaspoon salt; stir-fry 30 seconds. Add mushrooms, bamboo shoots and water chestnuts; stir-fry 1 minute. Stir in bok choy leaves, broth and wine; cover and cook 2 minutes. Stir in cornstarch mixture; cook and stir 15 seconds or until thickened. Add beef and pea pods; cook and stir 30 seconds or until beef is hot.

6 servings

Fresh water chestnuts are worth seeking out; they are becoming more available in supermarket produce departments and are so remarkably sweet and crunchy, they make the tedious peeling process seem very worthwhile. Chinese children eat them as snacks and have contests as to who can peel them fastest. Fresh water chestnuts must be washed thoroughly. Cut off the top, then peel the skin off.

STIR-FRIED BEEF AND TOMATOES

1-pound beef boneless sirloin or round steak
1 teaspoon vegetable oil
1 teaspoon cornstarch
1 teaspoon salt
⅛ teaspoon white pepper
3 medium tomatoes
1 small white onion
2 green onions (with tops)
3 tablespoons salted black beans
2 tablespoons cornstarch
1 tablespoon sugar
2 tablespoons water
2 tablespoons vegetable oil
2 tablespoons vegetable oil
1 teaspoon finely chopped gingerroot
1 teaspoon finely chopped garlic
½ cup Chicken Broth (page 47)

Trim fat from beef steak; cut beef lengthwise into 2-inch strips. Cut strips crosswise into ⅛-inch slices. Toss beef, 1 teaspoon vegetable oil, 1 teaspoon cornstarch, the salt and white pepper in medium bowl. Cover and refrigerate 30 minutes.

Cut each tomato into 8 wedges. Cut white onion into 1-inch squares. Cut green onions diagonally into 1-inch pieces. Place beans in small bowl; cover with warm water. Stir beans about 2 minutes to remove excess salt. Remove beans from water; drain well. Mix 2 tablespoons cornstarch, the sugar and water.

Heat wok until very hot. Add 2 tablespoons vegetable oil; tilt wok to coat side. Add beef; stir-fry 2 minutes or until beef is brown. Remove beef from wok.

Heat wok until very hot. Add 2 tablespoons vegetable oil; tilt wok to coat side. Add tomatoes, white onion, beans, gingerroot, and garlic; stir-fry 1 minute. Add broth; heat to boiling. Stir in cornstarch mixture; cook and stir 15 seconds or until thickened. Add beef and green onions; stir 30 seconds or until beef is hot.

4 or 5 servings

MANDARIN BEEF

1-pound beef boneless sirloin or round steak
1 tablespoon vegetable oil
2 teaspoons cornstarch
1 teaspoon salt
1 teaspoon soy sauce
½ teaspoon sugar
¼ teaspoon white pepper
2 green onions (with tops)
1 large green bell pepper
¼ cup vegetable oil
1 teaspoon finely chopped gingerroot
1 teaspoon finely chopped garlic
¾ cup shredded carrot
1 to 2 teaspoons chili paste
1 tablespoon dark soy sauce

Trim fat from beef steak; cut beef lengthwise into 2-inch strips. Cut strips crosswise into ⅛-inch slices. Stack slices and cut lengthwise into thin strips. Toss beef, 1 tablespoon vegetable oil, the cornstarch, salt, 1 teaspoon soy sauce, the sugar and white pepper in medium bowl. Cover and refrigerate 30 minutes.

Cut green onions diagonally into 2-inch pieces. Cut bell pepper into ⅛-inch strips.

Heat wok until very hot. Add ¼ cup vegetable oil; tilt wok to coat side. Add beef, gingerroot and garlic; stir-fry 3 minutes or until beef is brown. Add bell pepper, carrot and chili paste; stir-fry 1 minute. Stir in green onions and 1 tablespoon dark soy sauce; stir-fry 30 seconds.

4 servings

Stir-fried Beef and Tomatoes and Mandarin Beef

SHREDDED VEAL WITH GINGER

1-pound veal boneless steak
1 tablespoon cornstarch
½ teaspoon salt
⅛ tcaspoon white pepper
6 green onions (with tops)
1 tablespoon shredded gingerroot
½ teaspoon cornstarch
½ teaspoon sugar
1 tablespoon chicken broth
1 teaspoon light soy sauce
2 tablespoons vegetable oil

Trim fat from veal steak; cut veal lengthwise into 2-inch strips. Cut strips crosswise into ⅛-inch slices. Stack slices; cut lengthwise into thin strips. Toss veal, 1 tablespoon cornstarch, the salt and white pepper in medium bowl. Cover and refrigerate 30 minutes.

Cut green onions diagonally into 1-inch pieces. Mix ½ teaspoon cornstarch, the sugar, broth and soy sauce.

Heat wok until very hot. Add vegetable oil; tilt wok to coat side. Add veal and gingerroot; stir-fry 2 minutes or until veal turns white. Add green onions; stir-fry 10 seconds. Stir in cornstarch mixture; cook and stir 15 seconds or until thickened.

4 or 5 servings

MONGOLIAN LAMB

2-pound boneless leg of lamb
1 tablespoon cornstarch
1 tablespoon vegetable oil
2 teaspoons sugar
1 teaspoon salt
1 teaspoon white pepper
4 green onions (with tops)
3 tablespoons vegetable oil
1 teaspoon dried red pepper flakes
1 tablespoon brown bean sauce
2 teaspoons finely chopped garlic
1 teaspoon finely chopped gingerroot
2 teaspoons dark soy sauce

Trim fat from leg of lamb; cut lamb with grain into 2 × 1-inch strips. Cut strips across grain into ⅛-inch slices. Toss lamb, cornstarch, 1 tablespoon vegetable oil, the sugar, salt and white pepper in medium bowl. Cover and refrigerate 30 minutes. Cut green onions diagonally into 1-inch pieces.

Heat wok until very hot. Add 3 tablespoons vegetable oil; tilt wok to coat side. Add red pepper flakes, bean sauce, garlic and gingerroot; stir-fry 5 seconds. Add lamb; stir-fry 2 minutes or until brown. Add soy sauce and green onions; stir-fry 30 seconds.

4 servings

Shredded Veal with Ginger

6

漢字 (飯麵)

NOODLES AND RICE

NOODLES AND CHICKEN WITH PEANUT BUTTER SAUCE

2 whole chicken breasts (about 2 pounds)
Peanut Butter Sauce (page 108)
1 tablespoon vegetable oil
4 eggs, slightly beaten
2 quarts water
8 ounces fresh or dry egg noodles
2 teaspoons vegetable oil
2 green onions (with tops)
1 medium carrot
1 medium cucumber
¼ cup chopped peanuts

Place chicken breasts in 3-quart saucepan; add just enough water to cover chicken. Heat to boiling; reduce heat to medium. Cover and simmer 20 minutes or until chicken is no longer pink. Remove from heat; let stand covered 15 minutes. Remove chicken from broth. Remove bones and skin from chicken; cut chicken into 2-inch pieces. Pull pieces apart with grain to shred. Cover and refrigerate. Prepare Peanut Butter Sauce.

Heat wok until very hot. Add 1 teaspoon of the vegetable oil; tilt wok to coat side. Pour out excess oil. Add half of the eggs. Tilt wok to spread egg, forming a thin pancake. Fry egg until firm, turning once. Remove egg

from wok. Wash and thoroughly dry wok. Repeat with remaining oil and eggs. Cover and refrigerate fried eggs until cold.

Heat water to boiling in Dutch oven; stir in noodles. Heat to boiling; reduce heat to medium. Cook uncovered 5 minutes or until noodles are done; drain. Rinse in cold water; drain. Toss noodles with 2 teaspoons vegetable oil. (If using dry egg noodles, cook as directed on package.)

Cut onions into 2-inch pieces; shred lengthwise into fine strips. Cover with iced water; let stand 10 minutes or until strips curl.

Cut carrot into 2-inch pieces. Cut pieces lengthwise into ⅛-inch slices. Cut slices lengthwise into ⅛-inch strips. Place carrots in boiling water; heat to boiling; drain. Immediately rinse in cold water; drain. Cut cucumber lengthwise into halves; remove seeds. Cut halves crosswise into 2-inch pieces; cut each piece crosswise into ¼-inch strips.

Cut fried eggs into 1½ × ¼-inch strips. Mix 1 tablespoon sauce with chicken; 1 tablespoon sauce with carrot and 1 tablespoon sauce with cucumber. Toss remaining sauce with noodles until noodles are evenly coated. Place noodles on chilled platter. Place green onions on center on noodles. Arrange eggs, chicken, carrot and cucumber in spokes from green onions on noodles. Sprinkle with peanuts. Toss before serving.

5 to 6 servings

Noodles and Chicken with Peanut Butter Sauce

Peanut Butter Sauce

2 teaspoons dry mustard

2 teaspoons water

2 tablespoons plus 1½ teaspoons sesame oil

2 tablespoons peanut butter

2 tablespoons plus 1½ teaspoons water

2 tablespoons dark soy sauce

¼ cup red wine vinegar

2 tablespoons sugar

Stir dry mustard and 2 teaspoons water until smooth; reserve. Stir sesame oil into peanut butter until blended. Add 2 tablespoons plus 1½ teaspoons water; stir until blended. Add soy sauce; stir until blended. Add vinegar and sugar; stir until blended. Add reserved mustard; stir until blended. Cover and refrigerate.

STIR-FRIED NOODLES WITH SICHUAN SAUCE

6 medium dried black mushrooms

2 tablespoons cornstarch

2 tablespoons water

2 teaspoons red pepper sauce

2 quarts water

6 ounces Chinese egg noodles or linguini

2 tablespoons vegetable oil

2 tablespoons vegetable oil

10 ounces lean ground pork

2 tablespoons brown bean sauce

1 tablespoon finely chopped garlic

2 cups Chicken Broth (page 47)

2 teaspoons dark soy sauce

1 teaspoon sesame oil

2 tablespoons diced pimiento

1 tablespoon chopped green onion (with top)

Soak mushrooms in hot water 20 minutes or until soft; drain. Rinse in warm water; drain. Squeeze out excess moisture. Remove and discard stems; cut caps into ¼-inch pieces. Mix cornstarch, 2 tablespoons water and the pepper sauce.

Heat 2 quarts water to boiling in Dutch oven; stir in noodles. Heat to boiling; reduce heat to medium. Cook uncovered 5 minutes or until done; drain. Rinse in cold water; drain well. (If using linguini, cook as directed on package.)

Heat wok until very hot. Add 2 tablespoons vegetable oil; tilt wok to coat side. Reduce heat to medium. Add noodles; cook until light brown, using a fork to separate and flip noodles as they cook. (If noodles are not browning and appear to be dry, add 1 tablespoon vegetable oil.) Remove noodles to heatproof platter; keep warm in 300° oven.

Heat wok until very hot. Add 2 tablespoons vegetable oil; tilt wok to coat side. Add pork; stir-fry until pork is no longer pink. Add mushrooms, bean sauce and garlic; stir-fry 1 minute. Add broth; heat to boiling. Stir in cornstarch mixture; cook and stir until thickened. Stir in soy sauce, sesame oil and pimiento; cook and stir 15 seconds. Pour pork mixture over noodles; sprinkle with green onion.

4 servings

陳 *If you prefer less spicy recipes, reduce or omit the red pepper sauce. This is a very popular lunch dish in China. For a nice contrast of textures, serve it with Marinated Mushrooms and Cucumbers (page 35).*

Stir-fried Noodles with Sichuan Sauce

CANTONESE SEAFOOD CHOW MEIN

¼-pound walleye or sea bass fillets
½ teaspoon cornstarch
¼ teaspoon salt
1 teaspoon finely chopped gingerroot
Dash of white pepper
½ pound raw medium shrimp (in shells)
2 teaspoons finely chopped garlic
Dash of white pepper
6 medium dried black mushrooms
2 green onions (with tops)
4 ounces Chinese pea pods
6 large stalks bok choy
3 tablespoons oyster sauce
2 tablespoons cornstarch
2 tablespoons cold water
½ teaspoon sugar
½ teaspoon sesame oil
2 quarts water
6 ounces fresh or dry egg noodles
2 tablespoons vegetable oil
2 tablespoons vegetable oil
1 tablespoon vegetable oil
2 tablespoons dry white wine
½ teaspoon salt
1 cup Chicken Broth (page 47)

Pat fish dry; cut fish into 2 × ½-inch slices. Toss fish, ½ teaspoon cornstarch, ¼ teaspoon salt, the gingerroot and white pepper in medium bowl. Cover and refrigerate 30 minutes. Peel shrimp. Cut shrimp lengthwise into halves and wash out vein; pat dry. Toss shrimp, garlic and white pepper. Cover and refrigerate 20 minutes.

Soak mushrooms in hot water 20 minutes or until soft; drain. Rinse in warm water; drain. Squeeze out excess moisture. Remove and discard stems; cut caps into thin strips. Cut green onions into 2-inch pieces; shred lengthwise into fine strips. Cover with iced water; let stand 10 minutes or until strips curl.

Remove strings from pea pods; cut pea pods diagonally into halves. Place pea pods in boiling water. Cover and cook 1 minute; drain. Immediately rinse in cold water; drain. Remove leaves from bok choy stems. Cut leaves into 2-inch pieces; cut stems diagonally into ¼-inch slices (do not combine leaves and stems). Mix oyster sauce, 2 tablespoons cornstarch, 2 tablespoons water, the sugar and sesame oil.

Heat 2 quarts water to boiling in Dutch oven; stir in noodles. Heat to boiling; reduce heat to medium. Cook uncovered 5 minutes or until done; drain. Rinse in cold water; drain well. (If using dry egg noodles, cook as directed on package.)

Heat wok until very hot. Add 2 tablespoons vegetable oil; tilt wok to coat side. Reduce heat to medium. Add noodles; cook until light brown, using a fork to separate and flip noodles as they cook. (If noodles are not browning and appear to be dry, add 1 tablespoon vegetable oil.) Remove noodles to heatproof platter; keep warm in 300° oven.

Heat wok until very hot. Add 2 tablespoons vegetable oil; tilt wok to coat side. Add fish and shrimp; stir-fry until fish turns white and shrimp are pink. Remove fish mixture from wok; drain. Wash and thoroughly dry wok.

Heat wok until very hot. Add 1 tablespoon vegetable oil; tilt wok to coat side. Add mushrooms, bok choy stems, wine and ½ teaspoon salt; stir-fry 1 minute. Add chicken broth; heat to boiling. Cook uncovered 1 minute. Stir in bok choy leaves; heat to boiling. Stir in cornstarch mixture, cook and stir until thickened. Add pea pods; cook and stir 30 seconds. Add fish and shrimp; cook and stir until fish is hot. Pour seafood mixture over noodles; garnish with green onions.

Cantonese Seafood Chow Mein   *4 servings*

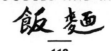
NOODLES WITH STIR-FRIED SHRIMP AND VEGETABLES

½ pound raw medium shrimp (in shells)
½ teaspoon cornstarch
¼ teaspoon salt
2 teaspoons finely chopped garlic
Dash of white pepper
6 medium dried black mushrooms
2 green onions (with tops)
1 pound broccoli
1 small head cauliflower
3 tablespoons oyster sauce
2 tablespoons cornstarch
2 tablespoons cold water
½ teaspoon sugar
½ teaspoon sesame oil
2 quarts water
6 ounces fresh or dry egg noodles
2 tablespoons vegetable oil
2 tablespoons vegetable oil
2 tablespoons vegetable oil
2 tablespoons dry white wine
½ teaspoon salt
1½ cups Chicken Broth (page 47)

Peel shrimp. Cut shrimp lengthwise into halves; wash out vein. Pat dry with paper towels. Toss shrimp with ½ teaspoon cornstarch, ¼ teaspoon salt, the garlic and white pepper. Cover and refrigerate 20 minutes.

Soak mushrooms in hot water 20 minutes or until soft; drain. Rinse in warm water; drain. Squeeze out excess moisture. Remove and discard stems; cut caps into thin strips. Cut green onions into 2-inch pieces; shred lengthwise into fine strips. Cover with iced water; let stand 10 minutes or until strips curl.

Cut broccoli lengthwise into 1-inch stems. Remove flowerets, keeping 1-inch stems. Cut stems diagonally into ¼-inch slices. Separate cauliflower into 1-inch flowerets. Place broccoli and cauliflower in boiling water; heat to boiling. Cook uncovered over high heat 3 minutes; drain. Immediately rinse in cold water; drain. Mix oyster sauce, 2 tablespoons cornstarch, 2 tablespoons water, the sugar and sesame oil.

Heat 2 quarts water to boiling in Dutch oven; stir in noodles. Heat to boiling; reduce heat to medium. Cook uncovered 5 minutes or until done; drain. Rinse in cold water; drain well. (If using dry egg noodles, cook as directed on package.)

Heat wok until very hot. Add 2 tablespoons vegetable oil; tilt wok to coat side. Reduce heat to medium. Add noodles; cook until light brown, using a fork to separate and flip noodles as they cook. (If noodles are not browning and appear to be dry, add 1 tablespoon vegetable oil.) Remove noodles to heatproof platter; keep warm in 300° oven.

Heat wok until very hot. Add 2 tablespoons vegetable oil; tilt wok to coat side. Add shrimp; stir-fry until shrimp are pink. Remove shrimp from the wok; drain. Wash and thoroughly dry wok.

Heat wok until very hot. Add 2 tablespoons vegetable oil; tilt wok to coat side. Add mushrooms, wine and ½ teaspoon salt; stir-fry 1 minute. Add broth; heat to boiling. Cook uncovered 1 minute. Stir in cornstarch mixture; cook and stir until thickened. Add broccoli and cauliflower; cook and stir 30 seconds. Stir in shrimp; cook and stir until shrimp are hot. Pour shrimp mixture over noodles; garnish with green onions.

4 servings

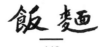
NOODLES WITH STIR-FRIED CHICKEN AND VEGETABLES

1 whole chicken breast (about 1 pound)
½ teaspoon cornstarch
¼ teaspoon salt
Dash of white pepper
6 medium dried black mushrooms
4 ounces Chinese pea pods
6 large stalks bok choy
3 tablespoons oyster sauce
2 tablespoons cornstarch
2 tablespoons cold water
½ teaspoon sugar
½ teaspoon sesame oil
2 quarts water
6 ounces fresh or dry egg noodles
2 tablespoons vegetable oil
2 tablespoons vegetable oil
2 teaspoons finely chopped garlic
1 teaspoon finely chopped gingerroot
1 tablespoon vegetable oil
1 teaspoon salt
½ cup sliced canned bamboo shoots
½ cup thinly sliced water chestnuts
1 cup Chicken Broth (page 47)

Remove bones and skin from chicken breast; cut chicken into thin slices. Mix chicken, ½ teaspoon cornstarch, ¼ teaspoon salt and the white pepper in medium bowl. Cover and refrigerate 30 minutes.

Soak mushrooms in hot water 20 minutes or until soft; drain. Rinse in warm water; drain. Squeeze out excess moisture. Remove and discard stems; cut caps into thin strips.

Remove strings from pea pods. Place pea pods in boiling water. Cover and cook 1 minute; drain. Immediately rinse in cold water; drain.

Remove leaves from bok choy stems. Cut leaves into 2-inch pieces; cut stems diagonally into ¼-inch slices (do not combine leaves and stems). Mix oyster sauce, 2 tablespoons cornstarch, 2 tablespoons water, the sugar and sesame oil.

Heat 2 quarts water to boiling in Dutch oven; stir in noodles. Heat to boiling; reduce heat to medium. Cook uncovered 5 minutes or until done, drain. Rinse in cold water; drain well. (If using dry egg noodles, cook as directed on package.)

Heat wok until very hot. Add 2 tablespoons vegetable oil; tilt wok to coat side. Reduce heat to medium. Add noodles; cook until light brown, using a fork to separate and flip noodles as they cook. (If noodles are not browning and appear to be dry, add 1 tablespoon vegetable oil.) Remove noodles to heatproof platter; keep warm in 300° oven.

Heat wok until very hot. Add 2 tablespoons vegetable oil; tilt wok to coat side. Add chicken, garlic and gingerroot; stir-fry until chicken turns white. Remove chicken from wok. Wash and thoroughly dry wok.

Heat wok until very hot. Add 1 tablespoon vegetable oil; tilt wok to coat side. Add bok choy stems, mushrooms and 1 teaspoon salt; stir-fry 1 minute. Stir in bamboo shoots, water chestnuts and broth; heat to boiling. Cook uncovered 1 minute. Stir in bok choy leaves; heat to boiling. Stir in cornstarch mixture; cook and stir until thickened. Add chicken and pea pods; cook and stir 30 seconds or until chicken is hot. Pour chicken mixture over noodles.

4 servings

SPINACH NOODLES WITH DICED PORK

¾-pound pork boneless loin
1 teaspoon cornstarch
½ teaspoon salt
Dash of white pepper
6 medium dried black mushrooms
1 green onion (with top)
2 tablespoons cornstarch
2 tablespoons water
1 teaspoon sugar
2 teaspoons dry white wine
2 teaspoons soy sauce
2 quarts water
6 ounces fresh or dry spinach noodles
2 tablespoons vegetable oil
2 tablespoons vegetable oil
1 teaspoon finely chopped gingerroot
1 teaspoon finely chopped garlic
1½ cups Chicken Broth (page 47)
2 tablespoons vegetable oil

Trim fat from pork loin; cut pork into ¼-inch pieces. Toss pork, 1 teaspoon cornstarch, the salt and white pepper in medium bowl. Cover and refrigerate 30 minutes.

Soak mushrooms in hot water 20 minutes or until soft; drain. Rinse in warm water; drain. Squeeze out excess moisture. Remove and discard stems; cut caps into ¼-inch pieces. Cut green onion diagonally into 1-inch pieces. Mix 2 tablespoons cornstarch, 2 tablespoons water and the sugar. Mix wine and soy sauce.

Heat 2 quarts water to boiling in Dutch oven; stir in noodles. Heat to boiling; reduce heat to medium. Cook uncovered 5 minutes or until done; drain. Rinse in cold water; drain well. (If using dry egg noodles, cook as directed on package.)

Heat wok until very hot. Add 2 tablespoons vegetable oil; tilt wok to coat side. Reduce heat to medium. Add noodles; cook until light brown, using a fork to separate and flip noodles as they cook. (If noodles are not browning and appear to be dry, add 1 tablespoon vegetable oil.) Remove noodles to heatproof platter; keep warm in 300° oven.

Heat wok until very hot. Add 2 tablespoons vegetable oil; tilt wok to coat side. Add pork, gingerroot and garlic; stir-fry 1 minute or until pork is no longer pink. Stir in soy sauce mixture. Remove pork from wok. Wash and thoroughly dry wok.

Heat mushrooms, broth and 2 tablespoons vegetable oil to boiling in wok; reduce heat to medium. Cover and cook 1 minute. Stir in cornstarch mixture; cook and stir until thickened. Add pork; cook and stir until pork is hot. Pour pork mixture over noodles; sprinkle with green onion.

4 servings

陳 *A symbol of longevity, noodles are required fare at birthday celebrations. For all Chinese noodle dishes, first boil the noodles and then rinse in cold water and drain well. The final cooking process—either stir-frying or deep-frying—adds flavor and texture. Only in northern China are noodles eaten for dinner. In the southern part of China, other than birthday celebrations, noodles are served for lunch or as a midnight snack.*

NOODLES WITH DICED VEAL AND MUSHROOMS

½-pound veal boneless round steak
1 teaspoon cornstarch
½ teaspoon salt
Dash of white pepper
6 medium dried black mushrooms
2 tablespoons cornstarch
2 tablespoons water
1 teaspoon sugar
2 quarts water
6 ounces fresh or dry egg noodles
2 tablespoons vegetable oil
2 tablespoons vegetable oil
1 teaspoon finely chopped gingerroot
1 teaspoon finely chopped garlic
2 teaspoons soy sauce
2 teaspoons dry white wine
1½ cups Chicken Broth (page 47)
1 tablespoon vegetable oil
1 green onion (with top), chopped

Trim fat from veal steak; cut veal into ¼-inch pieces. Toss veal with 1 teaspoon cornstarch, the salt and white pepper in medium bowl. Cover and refrigerate 30 minutes.

Soak mushrooms in hot water 20 minutes or until soft; drain. Rinse in warm water; drain.

Squeeze out excess moisture. Remove and discard stems; cut caps into ¼-inch pieces. Mix 2 tablespoons cornstarch, 2 tablespoons water and the sugar.

Heat 2 quarts water to boiling in Dutch oven; stir in noodles. Heat to boiling; reduce heat to medium. Cook uncovered 5 minutes or until noodles are done; drain. Rinse in cold water; drain well. (If using dry egg noodles, cook as directed on package.)

Heat wok until very hot. Add 2 tablespoons vegetable oil; tilt wok to coat side. Reduce heat to medium. Add noodles; cook until light brown, using a fork to separate and flip noodles as they cook. (If noodles are not browning and appear to be dry, add 1 tablespoon vegetable oil.) Remove noodles to heatproof platter; keep warm in 300° oven.

Heat wok until very hot. Add 2 tablespoons vegetable oil; tilt wok to coat side. Add veal, gingerroot and garlic; stir-fry 1 minute or until veal is done. Stir in soy sauce and wine. Remove veal from wok.

Heat mushrooms, broth and 1 tablespoon vegetable oil in wok to boiling; reduce heat to medium. Cover and cook 1 minute. Stir in cornstarch mixture; cook and stir until thickened. Add veal; cook and stir until veal is hot. Pour veal mixture over noodles; sprinkle with green onion.

4 servings

NOODLES WITH STIR-FRIED BEEF AND VEGETABLES

1-pound beef boneless sirloin or flank steak
1 teaspoon sugar
1 teaspoon cornstarch
1 teaspoon vegetable oil
½ teaspoon salt
Dash of white pepper
6 medium dried black mushrooms
2 green onions (with tops)
4 ounces Chinese pea pods
6 large stalks bok choy
3 tablespoons oyster sauce
2 tablespoons cornstarch
2 tablespoons cold water
½ teaspoon sugar
½ teaspoon sesame oil
2 quarts water
6 ounces fresh or dry egg noodles
2 tablespoons vegetable oil
2 tablespoons vegetable oil
1 tablespoon vegetable oil
2 tablespoons dry white wine
½ teaspoon salt
1 cup Chicken Broth (page 47)

Trim fat from beef steak; cut beef lengthwise into 2-inch strips. Cut strips crosswise into ⅛-inch slices. Toss beef, 1 teaspoon sugar, 1 teaspoon cornstarch, 1 teaspoon vegetable oil, ½ teaspoon salt and the white pepper in medium bowl. Cover and refrigerate 30 minutes.

Soak mushrooms in hot water 20 minutes or until soft; drain. Rinse in warm water; drain. Squeeze out excess moisture. Remove and discard stems; cut caps into thin strips. Cut green onions into 2-inch pieces; shred lengthwise into fine strips. Cover with iced water; let stand 10 minutes or until strips curl.

Remove strings from pea pods; cut pea pods diagonally into halves. Place pea pods in boiling water. Cover and cook 1 minute; drain. Immediately rinse in cold water; drain. Remove leaves from bok choy stems. Cut leaves into 2-inch pieces; cut stems diagonally into ¼-inch slices (do not combine leaves and stems). Mix oyster sauce, 2 tablespoons cornstarch, 2 tablespoons water, ½ teaspoon sugar and the sesame oil.

Heat 2 quarts water to boiling in Dutch oven; stir in noodles. Heat to boiling; reduce heat to medium. Cook uncovered 5 minutes or until done, drain. Rinse in cold water; drain well. (If using dry egg noodles, cook as directed on package.)

Heat wok until very hot. Add 2 tablespoons vegetable oil; tilt wok to coat side. Reduce heat to medium. Add noodles; cook until light brown, using a fork to separate and flip noodles as they cook. (If noodles are not browning and appear to be dry, add 1 tablespoon vegetable oil.) Remove noodles to heatproof platter; keep warm in 300 ° oven.

Heat wok until very hot. Add 2 tablespoons vegetable oil; tilt wok to coat side. Add beef; stir-fry 3 minutes or until beef is brown. Remove beef from wok. Wash and thoroughly dry wok.

Heat wok until very hot. Add 1 tablespoon vegetable oil; tilt wok to coat side. Add mushrooms, bok choy stems, wine and ½ teaspoon salt; stir-fry 1 minute. Add broth; heat to boiling. Cook uncovered 1 minute. Stir in bok choy leaves; heat to boiling. Stir in cornstarch mixture; cook and stir until thickened. Add pea pods; cook and stir 30 seconds. Add beef; cook and stir until beef is hot. Pour beef mixture over noodles; garnish with green onions.

4 servings

STIR-FRIED RICE NOODLES WITH VEGETABLES

6 medium dried black mushrooms
1 medium carrot
4 ounces Chinese pea pods
3 large stalks bok choy
3 green onions (with tops)
1 cup sliced canned bamboo shoots
1 tablespoon cornstarch
1 tablespoon water
8 ounces rice stick noodles
2 quarts water
2 tablespoons vegetable oil
2 teaspoons soy sauce
3 tablespoons vegetable oil
¾ cup Chicken Broth (page 47)

Soak mushrooms in hot water 20 minutes or until soft; drain. Rinse in warm water; drain. Squeeze out excess moisture. Remove and discard stems; cut caps into thin strips.

Cut carrot into 2-inch pieces. Cut pieces lengthwise into ⅛-inch slices. Cut slices lengthwise into ⅛-inch strips. Place carrots in boiling water. Heat to boiling; drain. Immediately rinse in cold water. Remove strings from pea pods. Place pea pods in boiling water. Cover and cook 1 minute; drain. Immediately rinse in cold water; drain. Cut each pea pod lengthwise into 3 or 4 strips.

Remove leaves from bok choy stems. Cut leaves into 2-inch pieces; cut stems diagonally into ¼-inch slices (do not combine leaves and stems). Cut green onions diagonally into 1½-inch pieces. Cut bamboo shoots lengthwise into thin strips. Mix cornstarch and 1 tablespoon water.

Pull noodles apart. Heat 2 quarts water to boiling; stir in noodles. Cook uncovered 1 minute; drain. Rinse in cold water; drain.

Heat wok until very hot. Add 2 tablespoons vegetable oil; tilt wok to coat side. Add noodles; stir-fry 2 minutes or until tender. Stir in soy sauce. Remove noodles from wok. Place on heatproof platter; keep warm in 300° oven.

Heat wok until very hot. Add 3 tablespoons vegetable oil; tilt wok to coat side. Add mushrooms, bok choy stems and bamboo shoots; stir-fry 1 minute. Add broth; heat to boiling. Stir in cornstarch mixture; cook and stir until thickened. Stir in carrot, pea pods, bok choy leaves and green onions; heat to boiling. Pour vegetable mixture over noodles.

4 servings

In this recipe, the rice noodles are boiled briefly before being stir-fried with soy sauce and then served topped with a variety of Chinese vegetables. Use a nonstick skillet if you don't have a wok, and toss the noodles continuously so they don't overcook.

RICE NOODLES WITH CURRIED SHRIMP

1 pound raw medium shrimp (in shells)
1 teaspoon finely chopped gingerroot
½ teaspoon cornstarch
¼ teaspoon salt
¼ teaspoon sesame oil
Dash of white pepper
1 pound celery cabbage
3 large green onions (with tops)
3 tablespoons cornstarch
3 tablespoons cold water
2 tablespoons dark soy sauce
Vegetable oil
4 ounces rice stick noodles
2 tablespoons vegetable oil
2 tablespoons curry powder
2 tablespoons vegetable oil
½ cup sliced canned bamboo shoots
1 cup Chicken Broth (page 47)

Peel shrimp. Cut shrimp lengthwise into halves; wash out vein. Toss shrimp, gingerroot, ½ teaspoon cornstarch, the salt, sesame oil and white pepper in medium bowl. Cover and refrigerate 20 minutes.

Cut celery cabbage into thin slices. Cut green onions diagonally into 2-inch pieces. Mix 3 tablespoons cornstarch, the water and soy sauce.

Heat vegetable oil (1½ inches) in wok to 425°. Pull noodles apart. Fry noodles, ¼ at a time 5 seconds or until puffed, turning once; drain on paper towels. Pour oil from wok; wash and thoroughly dry wok.

Heat wok until very hot. Add 2 tablespoons vegetable oil; tilt wok to coat side. Add shrimp; stir-fry until shrimp are pink. Add curry powder; stir-fry 30 seconds. Remove shrimp from the wok.

Heat wok until very hot. Add 2 tablespoons vegetable oil; tilt wok to coat side. Add celery cabbage and bamboo shoots; stir-fry 2 minutes. Stir in broth; heat to boiling. Stir in cornstarch mixture; cook and stir 10 seconds or until thickened. Add shrimp; cook and stir until shrimp are hot. Pour shrimp mixture over noodles; garnish with green onions.

4 to 6 servings

WHITE RICE

Place 2 cups long grain white rice in 2-quart saucepan. Add enough cold water to cover rice. Wash rice by rubbing rice gently between fingers; drain. Wash rice 5 or 6 times or until water is clear; drain. Add 2 cups cold water; heat to boiling. Cover tightly; reduce heat and simmer 20 minutes or until liquid is absorbed.

6 cups

陳 *It is the Chinese custom to rinse rice five or six times in large quantities of water before cooking to remove excess starch. This process results in the fresh-tasting, light-textured rice that is the backbone of Chinese cuisine. If not rinsed, the rice will clump and will not be as tender. White rice can be fully cooked ahead of time and refrigerated; reheat in the microwave or by steaming.*

Rice Noodles with Curried Shrimp

YOUNG JEWEL FRIED RICE

2 cups bean sprouts
2 tablespoons vegetable oil
3 eggs, slightly beaten
2 tablespoons vegetable oil
1 can (4 ounces) small button mushrooms,
    drained
1 teaspoon salt
3 tablespoons vegetable oil
4 cups White Rice (page 119)
3 tablespoons dark soy sauce
Dash of white pepper
1 cup chopped cooked shrimp
1 cup chopped Barbecued Pork (page 18)
½ cup frozen peas
¼ cup chopped green onions (with tops)

Rinse bean sprouts in cold water; drain.

Heat wok until very hot. Add 2 tablespoons vegetable oil; tilt wok to coat side. Add eggs; cook and stir until eggs are thickened throughout but still moist. Remove eggs from wok. Wash and thoroughly dry wok.

Heat wok until very hot. Add 2 tablespoons vegetable oil to wok; tilt to coat side. Add bean sprouts, mushrooms and salt; stir-fry 1 minute. Remove bean-sprout mixture from wok; drain.

Heat wok until very hot. Add 3 tablespoons vegetable oil to wok; tilt to coat side. Add rice; stir-fry 1 minute. Stir in soy sauce and white pepper. Stir in shrimp and pork. Add bean-sprout mixture, eggs, peas and green onions; stir-fry 30 seconds.

7 servings

This poetic description refers to the tender vegetables that add both color and flavor to the dish. Fried rice can be enhanced with whatever cooked meat you have on hand. "Young jewel" sounds like "Yeung Chau," a province in ancient China known for fried rice dishes.

STIR-FRIED RICE

1 cup bean sprouts
1 tablespoon vegetable oil
2 eggs, slightly beaten
1 tablespoon vegetable oil
1 jar (2½ ounces) sliced mushrooms, drained
2 tablespoons vegetable oil
3 cups White Rice (page 119)
2 tablespoons dark soy sauce
Dash of white pepper
1 cup cut-up Barbecued Pork (page 18) or
    cooked ham, chicken or turkey
2 green onions (with tops), chopped

Rinse bean sprouts in cold water; drain. Heat wok until very hot. Add 1 tablespoon vegetable oil; tilt wok to coat side. Add eggs; cook and stir until eggs are thickened throughout but still moist. Remove eggs from wok. Wash and thoroughly dry wok.

Heat wok until very hot. Add 1 tablespoon vegetable oil; tilt to coat side. Add bean sprouts and mushrooms; stir-fry 1 minute. Remove vegetables from wok; drain.

Heat wok until very hot. Add 2 tablespoons vegetable oil; tilt to coat side. Add rice; stir-fry 1 minute. Stir in soy sauce and white pepper. Stir in Barbecued Pork and green onions. Add eggs and vegetables; stir-fry 30 seconds.

4 servings

In the traditional Chinese diet, fried rice is strictly a snack, almost the equivalent of fast food; it's never served at a regular dinner or lunch because its flavorings might distract from, rather than enhance, the main course. Stir-fried Rice is a wonderful way to use leftover cooked rice. Start with a clean, hot wok and be sure the side is coated with oil. Reduce the heat as necessary to prevent the rice from burning. Stir-fried rice can be fully cooked ahead of time and refrigerated. Stir-fry when ready to serve.

CHICKEN FRIED RICE

1 whole chicken breast (about 1 pound)
½ teaspoon cornstarch
½ teaspoon salt
Dash of white pepper
1 cup bean sprouts
1 tablespoon vegetable oil
2 eggs, slightly beaten
2 tablespoons vegetable oil
1 jar (2½ ounces) sliced mushrooms, drained
½ teaspoon salt
2 tablespoons vegetable oil
3 cups White Rice (page 119)
1 or 2 tablespoons dark soy sauce
Dash of white pepper
2 green onions (with tops), chopped

Remove bones and skin from chicken breast; cut chicken into ¼-inch pieces. Toss chicken, cornstarch, ½ teaspoon salt and dash of white pepper. Rinse bean sprouts in cold water; drain.

Heat wok until very hot. Add 1 tablespoon vegetable oil; tilt wok to coat side. Add eggs; cook and stir until eggs are thickened throughout but still moist. Remove eggs from wok. Wash and thoroughly dry wok.

Heat wok until very hot. Add 2 tablespoons vegetable oil to wok; tilt to coat side. Add chicken; stir-fry until chicken turns white. Add bean sprouts, mushrooms and ½ teaspoon salt; stir-fry 1 minute. Remove chicken mixture from wok; drain.

Heat wok until very hot. Add 2 tablespoons vegetable oil to wok; tilt to coat side. Add rice; stir-fry 1 minute. Stir in soy sauce and white pepper. Add eggs, chicken mixture and green onions; stir-fry 30 seconds.

5 servings

7

蔬菜

VEGETABLES

STIR-FRIED EGGPLANT AND PEPPERS

1 medium eggplant
1 green bell pepper
1 red bell pepper
8 medium mushrooms
2 tablespoons oyster sauce
1 tablespoon sugar
3 tablespoons vegetable oil
2 teaspoons finely chopped garlic
1 teaspoon finely chopped gingerroot
1 teaspoon sesame oil

Pare eggplant if desired; cut into fourths and remove seeds. Cut into 2 × ¾ × ¼-inch strips. Cover with cold water; let stand 30 minutes. Drain; pat dry with paper towels. Cut bell peppers into ¼-inch strips. Cut mushrooms into ½-inch slices. Mix oyster sauce and sugar.

Heat wok until hot. Add vegetable oil; tilt wok to coat side. Add eggplant, garlic and gingerroot; stir-fry 1 minute. Add bell peppers and mushrooms; stir-fry 2 minutes. Add oyster sauce mixture and sesame oil; cook and stir 1 minute.

4 servings

ASPARAGUS WITH WATER CHESTNUTS

1 pound asparagus
3 ounces fresh mushrooms
2 shallots
1 tablespoon cornstarch
1 tablespoon cold water
3 tablespoons vegetable oil
1 cup sliced water chestnuts
½ cup Chicken Broth (page 47)
1 tablespoon oyster sauce
½ teaspoon salt

Break off tough ends of asparagus where stalks snap easily. Cut asparagus diagonally into 2-inch pieces. Cut mushrooms into ¼-inch slices. Cut shallots into fourths. Mix cornstarch and water.

Heat wok until very hot. Add vegetable oil; tilt wok to coat side. Add asparagus, mushrooms, shallots and water chestnuts; stir-fry 1 minute. Add broth, oyster sauce and salt; heat to boiling. Stir in cornstarch mixture; cook and stir until thickened.

4 servings

Stir-fried Eggplant and Peppers

STIR-FRIED ASPARAGUS WITH SICHUAN SAUCE

1 pound asparagus
1 teaspoon sugar
1 tablespoon chili paste
1 teaspoon sesame oil
2 tablespoons vegetable oil
1 teaspoon finely chopped garlic
¼ cup chicken broth
1 tablespoon vegetable oil
1 teaspoon finely chopped garlic
2 tablespoons Toasted Sesame Seed (page 34)

Break off tough ends of asparagus where stalks snap easily. Cut asparagus diagonally into 2-inch pieces. Mix sugar, chili paste and sesame oil.

Heat wok until very hot. Add 2 tablespoons vegetable oil; tilt wok to coat side. Add asparagus and 1 teaspoon garlic; stir-fry 1 minute. Add broth; cover and cook 2 minutes. Remove asparagus from wok; drain. Wash and throughly dry wok.

Heat wok until very hot. Add 1 tablespoon vegetable oil; tilt wok to coat side. Add 1 teaspoon garlic and the chili paste mixture; stir-fry 1 minute. Add asparagus; stir-fry 1 minute. Stir in sesame seed.

4 servings

Asparagus is rare and expensive in China, and so it is served on special occasions. Add chicken broth or water if necessary to avoid scorching the asparagus, but continue to stir-fry until the liquid has evaporated. If you want a milder dish, you can substitute ground bean sauce for the chili paste, but it won't be authentic Sichuan.

STIR-FRIED BOK CHOY WITH TOFU

8 large stalks bok choy
1-pound block firm tofu
2 tablespoons cornstarch
3 shallots
2 tablespoons vegetable oil
2 tablespoons oyster sauce
2 tablespoons vegetable oil
½ teaspoon salt

Remove leaves from bok choy stems. Cut leaves into 2-inch pieces; cut stems diagonally into ¼-inch slices (do not combine leaves and stems). Cut tofu into 1 × 1 × 1¼-inch pieces. Coat tofu with cornstarch. Cut shallots into thin slices.

Heat wok until very hot. Add 2 tablespoons vegetable oil; tilt wok to coat side. Add tofu; fry 2 pieces at a time 1 minute, turning once. Repeat with remaining tofu; return tofu to wok. Add oyster sauce; toss until tofu is evenly coated. Remove tofu from wok.

Heat wok until very hot. Add 2 tablespoons vegetable oil; tilt wok to coat side. Add shallots; stir-fry 30 seconds. Add bok choy stems and salt; stir-fry 1 minute. Add tofu and bok choy leaves; cover and cook 1 minute over high heat.

4 servings

Tofu, that culinary chameleon, takes on the exotic flavor of oyster sauce and shallots here. Dusting the tofu cubes with cornstarch makes them easier to handle and produces a firm, crisp exterior. Add the fragile bok choy leaves at the last minute to avoid overcooking. If not using a wok, use a saucepan or skillet with high sides. Tofu is very moist, and oil may spatter.

Stir-fried Bok Choy with Tofu

STIR-FRIED JICAMA WITH BLACK MUSHROOMS

8 medium dried black mushrooms
4 shallots
3 stalks celery
8 ounces jicama
3 tablespoons vegetable oil
¼ teaspoon salt
¼ cup chicken broth
¼ teaspoon sugar

Soak mushrooms in hot water 20 minutes or until soft; drain. Rinse in warm water; drain. Squeeze out excess moisture. Remove and discard stems; cut caps into ¼-inch slices. Cut shallots into fourths. Cut celery diagonally into ¼-inch slices. Pare jicama and cut into 2-inch wide pieces; cut into ¼-inch slices.

Heat wok until very hot. Add 3 tablespoons vegetable oil; tilt wok to coat side. Add mushrooms, shallots, celery and salt; stir-fry 1 minute. Add broth and sugar; cook and stir 1 minute or until all moisture has evaporated. Add jicama; cook and stir 1 minute.

4 servings

ZUCCHINI AND POTATOES IN CURRY SAUCE

4 small zucchini (about 16 ounces)
2 medium potatoes (about 10 ounces)
1 medium tomato
1 small onion
¼ cup vegetable oil
2 teaspoons finely chopped garlic
1 tablespoon curry powder
2 teaspoons dark soy sauce
1 teaspoon sugar

Cut zucchini into ¾-inch pieces. Cut potatoes into ¾-inch pieces. Place tomato in boiling water; boil 30 seconds. Immediately rinse in cold water. Peel tomato; cut into ½-inch pieces. Cut onion into ½-inch pieces.

Heat wok until very hot. Add ¼ cup vegetable oil; tilt wok to coat side. Reduce heat to medium. Add potatoes; stir-fry about 4 minutes or until light brown. Remove potatoes from wok with slotted spoon; drain on paper towels.

Heat remaining oil in wok until hot. Add onion, garlic and curry powder; stir-fry until onion is tender. Add zucchini and tomato; stir-fry 2 minutes. Add potatoes, soy sauce and sugar; stir-fry 1 minute.

4 servings

 Curry is an Indian flavoring, not traditionally Chinese, but Chinese cooks have been making their own version of curry powder since about 1900. Adding soy sauce makes the dish uniquely Far Eastern. It is important that curry powder be cooked (rather than added after cooking) to bring out the rich flavor of this spice mixture.

Zucchini and Potatoes in Curry Sauce and Stir-fried Jicama with Black Mushrooms

SWEET-AND-SOUR CABBAGE

1 medium head cabbage (about 1 pound)
4 shallots
1 tablespoon cornstarch
1 tablespoon water
3 tablespoons vegetable oil
¼ cup ketchup
3 tablespoons sugar
1 teaspoon salt
1 teaspoon red pepper sauce
½ cup Chicken Broth (page 47)

Cut cabbage into 1½-inch pieces. Cut shallots into fourths. Mix cornstarch and water.

Heat wok until very hot. Add vegetable oil; tilt wok to coat side. Add cabbage; stir-fry 1 minute. Add shallots, ketchup, sugar, salt and pepper sauce; stir-fry 1 minute. Add broth; heat to boiling. Stir in cornstarch mixture; cook and stir 10 seconds or until thickened.

4 servings

STEAMED TOFU HOME STYLE

1-pound block firm tofu
1 green onion (with top)
2 tablespoons vegetable oil
1 teaspoon finely chopped gingerroot
1 tablespoon dark soy sauce
1 teaspoon sesame oil
½ teaspoon sugar

Cut tofu into 2 × 2 × ½-inch pieces. Cut green onion diagonally into ½-inch pieces.

Place tofu on shallow heatproof platter. Place platter on rack in steamer; cover and steam over boiling water 10 minutes. (Add boiling water if necessary.) Pour off excess water from platter.

Heat 8-inch skillet until hot. Add vegetable oil; tilt skillet to coat side. Add gingerroot; cook and stir gingerroot until light brown (be careful not to burn). Stir in soy sauce, sesame oil and sugar. Pour over tofu; garnish with green onion.

4 servings

TOFU WITH BARBECUE SAUCE

1-pound block firm tofu
2 tablespoons cornstarch
½ cup Chicken Broth (page 47)
1 tablespoon cornstarch
1 teaspoon sugar
1 teaspoon dark soy sauce
1 cup vegetable oil
2 tablespoons vegetable oil
2 tablespoons Hoisin sauce
2 teaspoons finely chopped garlic

Cut tofu into ½-inch slices; coat both sides of slices with the 2 tablespoons cornstarch. Mix broth, 1 tablespoon cornstarch, the sugar and soy sauce.

Heat 1 cup vegetable oil to 350° in wok. Fry tofu, 2 slices at a time, until light brown; drain on paper towels. Repeat with remaining tofu. Cool 5 minutes; cut each slice into 4 triangles. Place tofu on shallow platter. Pour oil out of wok.

Heat wok until very hot. Add 2 tablespoons vegetable oil; tilt wok to coat side. Add Hoisin sauce and garlic; stir-fry 15 seconds. Stir in cornstarch mixture; heat to boiling. Pour barbecue sauce over tofu.

4 servings

STIR-FRIED GREEN BEANS WITH SICHUAN SAUCE

1 pound green beans
2 teaspoons dark soy sauce
2 teaspoons finely chopped garlic
1 teaspoon sugar
1 teaspoon sesame oil
2 teaspoons chili paste
3 tablespoons vegetable oil
¼ cup chicken broth
2 tablespoons Toasted Sesame Seed (page 34)

Cut green beans diagonally into 2-inch length. Mix soy sauce, garlic, sugar, sesame oil and chili paste.

Heat wok until very hot. Add vegetable oil; tilt wok to coat side. Add green beans; stir-fry 1 minute. Add broth; cover and cook 5 minutes. Add soy sauce mixture; stir-fry until green beans are coated and moisture is evaporated. Stir in sesame seed.

4 servings

 Try this recipe with long beans, available in Chinese specialty stores. They resemble western green beans in flavor but are a bit crunchier; they're also over a foot long. If you can't find them, fresh green beans will be just as delicious.

BRAISED MUSHROOMS WITH LETTUCE

15 medium dried black mushrooms
1 small head iceberg lettuce (about 8 ounces)
1 tablespoon cornstarch
1 tablespoon water
1 teaspoon sugar
½ teaspoon salt
¼ cup vegetable oil
1 cup Chicken Broth (page 47)
2 tablespoons soy sauce
1 teaspoon sesame oil

Soak mushrooms in hot water 20 minutes or until soft; drain. Rinse in warm water; drain. Squeeze out excess moisture. Remove and discard stems; cut caps into ½-inch strips. Separate lettuce into leaves. Mix cornstarch, water, sugar and salt.

Heat wok until very hot. Add vegetable oil; tilt wok to coat side. Add mushrooms; stir-fry 30 seconds. Add broth, soy sauce and sesame oil; heat to boiling. Reduce heat to medium; cover and cook 10 minutes. Remove mushrooms, using slotted spoon, from broth; reserve.

Heat broth to boiling over high heat. Add lettuce; cook uncovered 2 minutes. Remove lettuce from broth, using slotted spoon; place on shallow platter.

Add reserved mushrooms to broth; heat to boiling. Stir in cornstarch mixture; cook and stir until thickened. Pour mushroom mixture over lettuce.

4 servings

FUN SEE VEGETABLES

6 medium dried black mushrooms

2 ounces cellophane noodles (bean thread)

½ ounce tiger lily buds

4 large stalks bok choy

4 ounces Chinese pea pods

4-ounce block firm tofu

2 green onions (with tops)

2 tablespoons vegetable oil

3 tablespoons vegetable oil

1 teaspoon finely chopped gingerroot

1 teaspoon salt

½ cup sliced canned bamboo shoots

½ cup sliced water chestnuts

½ cup water

2 tablespoons dark soy sauce

½ teaspoon sesame oil

Soak mushrooms in hot water 20 minutes or until soft; drain. Rinse in warm water; drain. Squeeze out excess moisture. Remove and discard stems; cut caps into ½-inch pieces. Soak noodles in warm water 5 minutes; drain. Cut noodles into 4-inch pieces. Soak tiger lily buds in warm water about 5 minutes or until soft; drain. Remove and discard tips.

Cut bok choy stems (with leaves) diagonally into ½-inch slices. Remove strings from pea pods. Place pea pods in boiling water. Cover and cook 1 minute; drain. Immediately rinse in cold water; drain. Cut tofu into halves; cut each half into ¼-inch slices. Cut green onions diagonally into 2-inch pieces.

Heat wok until very hot. Add 2 tablespoons vegetable oil; tilt wok to coat side. Add tofu; stir-fry carefully 1 minute. Remove tofu from wok. Wash and thoroughly dry wok.

Heat wok until very hot. Add 3 tablespoons vegetable oil; tilt wok to coat side. Add mushrooms, tiger lily buds, bok choy, gingerroot and salt; stir-fry 1 minute. Add bamboo shoots and water chestnuts; stir-fry 1 minute.

Stir in water; heat to boiling. Add noodles and pea pods; cook and stir 30 seconds. Add tofu, green onions and soy sauce; cook and stir 30 seconds. Stir in sesame oil.

5 servings

ZUCCHINI WITH SALTED BLACK BEANS AND CHILIES

¼ cup salted black beans

4 small zucchini (about 16 ounces)

2 hot green chilies

2 green onions (with tops)

¼ cup chicken broth

1 tablespoon cornstarch

1 teaspoon sugar

3 tablespoons vegetable oil

2 teaspoons finely chopped garlic

Place beans in small bowl; cover with warm water. Stir beans about 2 minutes to remove excess salt. Remove beans from water; drain well. Cut zucchini into 2 × ½-inch strips. Remove seeds and membranes from chilies. Finely chop chilies. Cut green onions diagonally into 1-inch pieces. Mix broth, cornstarch and sugar.

Heat wok until very hot. Add vegetable oil; tilt wok to coat side. Add beans, chili peppers and garlic; stir-fry 20 seconds. Add zucchini; stir-fry 2 minutes. Stir in cornstarch mixture; cook and stir until thickened. Add green onions; cook and stir 15 seconds.

4 servings

MENUS

Lunch

Each menu serves 4 to 6

Wonton Soup

Chicken-Pineapple Salad

Stir-fried Rice

Barbecued Pork

Marinated Mushrooms and Cucumbers

Marinated Broccoli

Stir-fried Rice Noodles with Vegetables or Stir-fried Rice

Pot Stickers

Crabmeat Salad

Barbecued Pork Bao

Dinner

Each menu serves 4 to 6

Shrimp-Tofu Ball Soup

Coconut Chicken

Stir-fried Beef and Asparagus

White Rice or Stir-fried Rice

Stir-fried Wontons with Sichuan Sauce or Shrimp Toast

Chinese Chicken Salad

Sweet-and-Sour Pork

Young Jewel Fried Rice

Barbecued Chicken Wings

Shrimp Toast

Kung Pao Pork

Chicken Fried Rice

Crabmeat Puffs or Shrimp Toast

Crabmeat Salad

Fried Shrimp with Red Sauce

Asparagus with Water Chestnuts

White Rice

Special Occasions
Each menu serves 10 to 12

Chilled Spring Rolls

Crispy Scallops

Bean Sprout Salad

Crabmeat Salad

Clams with Salted Black Beans and Chilies

Glazed Walleye

Stir-fried Shrimp with Vegetables

White Rice

Sichuan Chicken Dumplings

Egg Rolls

Chicken-Papaya Salad

Lemon Chicken

Kung Pao Shrimp

Chicken Fried Rice

Shrimp Toast

Chicken Wing Drumsticks

Barbecued Ribs

Lotus Root Salad

Sesame Pork

Spicy Chicken with Broccoli

Noodles with Stir-fried Beef and Vegetables

Special Occasions Menu 1 (Left to right from bottom): Crispy Scallops, Chilled Spring Rolls, Glazed Walleye, Bean Sprout Salad, Crabmeat Salad, Clams with Salted Black Beans and Chilies and Stir-fried Shrimp with Vegetables

INDEX